MY CHILD ON DRUGS?

YOUTH AND THE DRUG CULTURE

BY ART LINKLETTER
AND GEORGE GALLUP, JR.

 STANDARD PUBLISHING
Cincinnati, Ohio   5015

Library of Congress Cataloging in Publication Data

Linkletter, Art, 1912-
    My Child on Drugs?
    1. Youth—United States—Drug use. 2. Linkletter, Diane, 1949-1969.
Narcotic addicts—United States—Biography. 4. Narcotic addicts—United
States—Family relationships. 5. Marijuana. 6. Substance abuse—United
States. I. Gallup, George, 1930-   joint author. II. Title.
HV5824.Y68L56   362.2'9'088055   81-50355
ISBN 0-87239-456-5   AACR2

Foreword

In the survey conducted in 1980 for the White House Conference on Families by the Gallup Organization, alcohol and drug abuse repeatedly reared its ugly head. For example, named most frequently as most harmful to family life among a list of 11 items is "drug abuse" (59 percent), "alcohol abuse" (60 percent), "a decline in religious and moral values" (40 percent), and "poverty" (29 percent).

One person in seven (14 percent) says that alcohol and drug abuse (from a list of 14 items) is one of the three biggest problems facing their families today.

One-fourth of all survey respondents (23 percent) believe alcohol or drug abuse (from a list of 12 items) is one of the three reasons most responsible for the high divorce rate in the United States.

Of particular importance are the views and habits of the 25 million teenagers who will shape the future of our society. A recent (1980) Gallup Youth Survey found that the number of teens who view marijuana smoking as a very big problem has jumped by 12 percent over a 1978 survey, in which only one teen in four saw pot smoking in the same light. In addition, while teens in the 1978 survey put classroom disturbances at the top of a list of eight disciplinary problems, our most recent poll found marijuana smoking replacing such disturbances as the biggest problem of the eight.

Following those two problems in the eyes of teens contacted in our latest poll are, in order, theft, vandalism, drinking, fighting, the use of hard drugs and weapons. Drinking and hard drug use also showed hefty increases in the most recent survey.

The two key reasons given by teens to explain why persons their age use alcohol and drugs are peer pressure and to escape from the pressures of society and life.

Here is the full list:

WHY ARE YOUNG PEOPLE USING ALCOHOL/DRUGS?
(Views of teenagers)

Peer pressure; conformity; "it's the thing"	29%
Escape from pressures of society/life	26%
To have a good time; to feel good; for "kicks"	15%
Problems at home, with family	11%
Showing off; "to be cool"; "act big"; be popular	10%
To act "grown up"; to imitate adults	8%
Boredom	2%
Rebellion	2%
Parental indifference	1%
Other reasons	2%
Don't know/no answer	9%
	115%*

Totals add to more than 100% due to multiple responses.

If America cherishes the family, and the White House Conference on Family (WHCF) study clearly shows that we do, we must take steps to deal with the factors most responsible for the destruction of the family—alcohol and drug abuse.

I would like to suggest a five-part plan for ministers and other church leaders:

1. Encourage parents to discuss drinking/drug problems with their children.
2. Attend a good workshop on alcohol/drug abuse.
3. Speak openly about the subject.
4. Establish a team program with parents so the church and family can reinforce one another.
5. Stress religious reasons for abstinence.

George Gallup, Jr.

Contents

PART ONE: The Story

My Daughter
DIANE

"The grief of parents is private," so said Frances Bacon some 300 years ago. But my wife and I agreed to bare our grief and outrage, to help other kids.

The world has changed a lot since the days when I enjoyed hosting the daily TV show that featured "kids saying the darndest things."

Kids have always been my thing, and I sometimes wonder what has become of all the cute youngsters who made that show. I'll never know. I do know what happened to one adorable little girl who grew up here in the Los Angeles area. She was my daughter Diane—and she died just before her twentieth birthday, a victim of the drug society.

I couldn't count the times I've been asked, "Did your daughter commit suicide?"

Did she? As far as we know, it was either suicide or some extraordinary reaction to a frantic bewildered dismay or syndrome that comes from a flashback episode with LSD.

Diane was not a drug addict but, growing up in the sixties, she went out to parties where there were many kinds of drugs around. They were what is called "Spree" or "Recreational" drugs. What does that mean? Well, it's like when people who would never drink at home—they're not drinkers—but if they're at a party and everybody's having a drink, they'll take one or two. They'd never go to a bar and drink, but they'll go along with it at a party. Well, Diane was the kind of girl like many others who had the problem of being a celebrity's kid, so she really would strive to be one of the crowd. So, though I'm quite sure she was not wallowing in drugs, she was one of those kids who had taken just enough so that she became a victim of the flashback syndrome. Let me explain what this is: after the initial LSD trip there's a recurrence. It can come a day, a week, even up to a year later. It's a kind of time bomb that can be triggered by a number of things, maybe an extraordinary sound on radio or TV, or flashing pictures—even a traffic light. We didn't know it then, but we do know now that Diane had been experiencing some flashbacks, and she thought she was in danger of losing her mind. She was an extremely bright, very sensitive girl.

The day she died, she was in her own apartment, which we had consented for her to have, cooking dinner for a friend. What happened? We'll never know. Her brother had a call from her that scared him so that he hurried right over to be with her. But he was too late. She had been perfectly all right five minutes before. But something happened—and she went out the window of a six-story apartment building, a victim of what I've come to call "the Russian roulette of drugs."

Taking LSD is like dropping sand into a computer. It throws off the intricate balances of the mind. And at that time, LSD was being touted by Timothy Leary as a mind-opener and expander, a kind of religious experience, a gift from God.

So there was my Diane, a girl from a Christian family, a family that didn't drink, didn't smoke—we've hardly taken an aspirin in years. There was love and understanding, no split in our family. We lived a moderate life, not flaunting the material things we have. We've spent time together as a family, gone on backpacking trips into the High Sierras every summer. We did all the things the books say you should do as a family.

In spite of all of that, Diane died. She was a chance-taker, and *she was one of those for whom LSD is poison.*

I've talked with kids who've taken LSD ten, twenty, maybe a hundred times with no perceptible damage. I know some who have partially freaked out, some who are freaked out permanently—and of course, many who have died. It was the "acid rock" period. The drug scene was exciting and glamorous and popular to these kids. Not so different, really, although more disastrous, than the

10

things we did when I was growing up. Like most of my young friends, I'd sneak out behind the garage and smoke a cigarette. That was the way of showing a kid's independence—a little rebellion—a bit of risk-taking. Every kid growing up takes chances, usually glorying in the risk. Sometimes I tell the amusing story of the distraught mother who looked out the back door to see her little guy high up on a tree limb and she yells at him, "Jimmy, if you fall out of that tree and break your arm I'll—I'll *kill* you!' "

Kids like to do things like that. They go walking on the railroad tracks in defiance of the chance that a train might thunder along. They swim in places they know they shouldn't. I know of a mother who said regularly, "I wouldn't be able to sleep a wink at night if I thought my John went swimming in that old quarry" (an abandoned quarry that had filled spontaneously and had been plumbed at 90 feet). Well, that mother would have been a total insomniac, for her John dived in that water every chance he had. This is all part of growing up. And a certain number of the risk-takers are going to die. A boy I know died in this way just last weekend, the day before his graduation from high school. Having a fun day with his friends at an amusement park, he got out of a moving car on a ride, and was crushed to death.

Back to Diane. What did her death do to me, to her mother, to us as a family? Did we seek to hide and to keep the facts from the press and the everpresent media? No. There was no carpet wide enough or long enough to sweep it under, even if the thought had occurred to me. I just wanted to lash out, to kill the Timothy Learys who drove kids to drugs like a streetlight draws moths. I was *mad*. I was determined to do something, even if it cost me my life, to stop this trafficking in dope that was threatening the lives and future of any kid who was tempted to the flame.

One of the things that made me totally unprepared for what happened to Diane was her own public attitude towards drugs. I had suspected that she and her brother and sister had experimented with smoking pot or some such thing, because I don't know of any kids around Hollywood who live a sophisticated life who haven't tried it. And I WARNED THEM. But, just a couple of weeks or so before her death, Diane had returned from a nationwide tour, a series of personal appearances as an endorser for a wristwatch company based in New York. And, along the way, many of the hosts of the show would ask her for her thinking about the younger generation, and in particular what she thought of drug use and

11

abuse. As a result, I received letters and phone calls from people all over the country congratulating me on having such a levelheaded, sweet, sensible daughter who spoke out against the drug syndrome. Basically, this is how she felt. She didn't need any drugs; she had everything going for her. She had a contract with Warner Brothers, and was about to start filming. She and I had just made a record called, "We Love You, Call Collect." It was a talk record designed to encourage runaways to call their parents, collect. It promised no lectures, no putdowns for the kid who would heed the parents' appeal and call home. And this record won the Grammy Award for the best talking record of the year.

So you see, Diane and I had a lot of things going. She was not a desperate or lonely or defeated girl, no stereotype of the one who seeks release and relief through drugs or through taking her own life. She had no known reason whatsoever, except it was part of the sixties—and I am sorry to say, it is part of the eighties.

People have asked me, "Do you think the drug scene is strictly an accidental convergence of events, or is there possibly some conspiratorial manipulation by some groups involved?"

It would be easy to blame somebody or some group. And I do occasionally run into people who say, "It's the Communists; they're out to ruin our youth in this country," etc. I say, "I wish to God it were." It would ease Diane's death for me. But that is not so; it's our fault. It is a convergence of events and philosophies as I see it— perhaps we can say it's society's fault if we want to stoop to faultfinding to salve our personal and national consciences.

I believe it's the conflicting values and the violence our young people were exposed to with nothing really to counteract it in their minds. Since the assassination of President John F. Kennedy, we've had a series of hammer blows in these United States. After the death of President Kennedy, came the assassination of his brother Robert, then Dr. Martin Luther King, stunning the nation and stirring up red-hot emotions. The Civil Rights riots, deaths, and marches followed. Then there were the campus revolts, the burning of buildings, and the kidnapping of the Deans.

On top of this simmering mess of terribly divisive happenings that upset so many, came the tragic Vietnamese War which split the country. As never before, a generation gap sharply divided young and older. The loyal "My country, right or wrong," was challenged by the kids crying, "Our country has no right to send us anywhere to fight!"

12

The whole cauldron brewed, then spewed out the sentiments of, "Live now. You may not be around tomorrow."

Ours was just one of the homes that found "drugs on our doorstep," and a loved daughter dead just when life had so much left to offer her.

My anger was sheer blind rage. But it had no direction. I just felt the need to hit back. I couldn't leave the issue alone then—and I can't now. The difference is that since then I've learned that vengeance is not mine.

As might be expected, the news of Diane's death brought a great volume of letters to us. Of all that flood of mail, one letter still stands out, for it changed the course of action I might otherwise have taken; not that it made me simmer down one bit, but it gave me a constructive route to take.

The writer was a man I had long admired for his sensitivity and his awareness of what people need. His name is Dr. Norman Vincent Peale.

There had been other though far less traumatic times in my life when I was confused and didn't know quite which way to go. And each time, somehow I got a sense that "This is the way; walk ye in it." I knew the guidance came from God, and each instance served to underscore my basic often-tested belief that ultimately, if we will await His time, God's way will make sense.

So, while I was reading the words written by Dr. Peale, I had the strong conviction that again, despite my hatred and vengeful spirit, God was speaking to me.

Dr. Peale, after expressing his sincere sympathy for us, went on to urge me to think through with him the meaning of Diane's death. He sensed the emptiness I felt, and the fact that my dwelling on how my daughter had died would just make me all the more bitter and vindictive. He suggested that her death was not in vain, that it could serve to give new meaning and purpose to my own life.

He said Diane's life—and death—could change the way I lived.

The grief was still there, the hurt had not diminished, but a new sense of purpose began to draw out the poison from my mind. And in its place, a new vigor to take sensible, constructive action emerged.

To be sure, the godly minister was counseling me from his own profound compassion and faith; yet I'm equally sure that it was God's wisdom, not Norman Vincent Peale's, that broke through the bitterness and gave me new motivation. This undoubtedly saved my sanity. It sent me out on a campaign, and I'm still on it today.

As I expressed in dedicating to Diane my book, *Drugs at My Door Step,* "With the ending of her life, a new life began for me. I have dedicated my efforts in the crusade against drug abuse to making her existence meaningful through the saving of others." And I would reiterate, if I had known earlier what I am putting into this book, my daughter Diane might be alive today.

I'm still haunted at times by the letters that have come to me saying, "We know how you feel because this terrible thing is happening to us, too. We're frantic. We don't know what to do or which way to turn. Please help us!" I'll share just a couple.

From a small town in Pennsylvania:

Our son, a first year medical student, took LSD after much coaxing by "friends" and out of curiosity. Little happened the day he took the drug. But a week later, driving on the Penn Turnpike, he had a recurrence.

He brought his car to a stop, stripped completely, folded his clothes neatly, got out of the car feeling that he could outrace, barefooted, anything on that concrete highway.

A camper hit him and hurled him into the air. He suffered a partly crushed skull, and only after a long month of anguish were we given any hope that he would make it back. He has lost the sight of one eye and has a silver plate in his head. Perhaps someday he may resume his studies. Perhaps not.

Another, so typical, so sad came from a small town in the Pacific Northwest:

My daughter left home on the night of July 8; I've neither seen nor heard from her since. I hadn't the slightest idea she was on drugs; now I know she was. What caused her to run away, and where is she? She did not take any clothes but what she had on. Sometimes I think I will lose my mind. I go into her room. There's her billford, her skis, the jewelry box her brother brought her from Vietnam. Why? Why did she feel she had to leave? I can't find any answer. She would have been 18 this November.

As one woman wrote me whose son had died of an overdose of heroin, "It's like having one word tattooed across your heart: WHY?"

Experts still grope for reasons, for answers to that won't-go-away *why.* Some rationalize that ours is a pill-oriented society—and it is. Others submit that our affluent youth can afford to disregard the traditional American values of discipline and self-denial; that it is natural for young people to seek thrills, and rebel against authority (as I've said earlier in this chapter). No doubt there is some truth in all of these theories. Yet the question remains.

So I would say to parents everywhere, take off the blinders; face up to the fact, ugly though it is, that sooner or later it may be *your* child who is offered marijuana, barbiturates, amphetamines, LSD, or other illegal drugs. And these will be offered under enticing circumstances, most likely by a member of his own peer group. Your son will be urged to try glue sniffing, teased as a coward if he doesn't. Your daughter will be urged to try diet pills or sleeping pills taken from some family medicine cabinet. "Getting a little high," she'll be told, "is harmless and the 'in' thing to do."

You can't watch your children 24 hours a day. You can try to build a relationship with the child that will form a protective barrier between him and the drug menace. I'm not saying you will succeed; in spite of your best efforts, you may fail. But you will know you've tried—and believe me, this knowledge in itself may save your own sanity.

Spend more time with your kids. Talk with them more, around the dinner table, when you're driving along in the car, whenever they appear to be relaxed with you and receptive to what you're talking about. You must be sensitive to the right moment. You can't barge in with, "Now we're going to talk about drug abuse," and expect to get anywhere. They need to know that you are interested in them, that you trust them, expect the best of them. But don't be complacent, assuming that everything's all right.

In Diane's case, I think in retrospect that we underestimated the impact of a highly sophisticated, thrill-seeking environment on a sensitive, adventurous, high-strung girl. There was never any breakdown of communication. Even after she had her own apartment, we kept in touch. But often, I think now, what she told me was what she knew I wanted to hear. And that cracks me up even today.

What would make a teenage daughter feel she had to monitor what she told her dad?

Could it be that she sensed, *If I speak about certain things—if I talk freely about anything that's on my mind, I don't quite know how Dad would react?* Was there something about my attitude, unknown to me, that made her feel I might be judgmental? I'll never know. What I have to live with is the knowledge that caught in a net from which she wasn't able to extricate herself, my daughter didn't turn to her father for help.

So, dads, while you still have your daughters, go to work on this.

15

Don't let the catch-all word "communication" deter you. Get in there and be a part of your daughter's life. Listen—capital L—*listen*. Encourage her to share her hopes and dreams and longings and aspirations. Let her talk. Be enthusiastic about her interests. Actually, a lot of what I'm suggesting is a practical outworking of the Golden Rule. Listen and interact with your child as you would want someone to do with you. This means listening without being impatient for your turn to say what you're thinking about instead of really listening. Kids have a kind of radar for sensing when adults aren't really interested in them. This breeds cynicism and a disregard for adults in general. It's not easy to pay 100% attention, but it pays off.

The truth is that most teenagers do not have one adult to talk to who genuinely cares a hoot about what they are thinking or saying.

I heard a kid bragging one day about her dad. Her eyes shone as she asserted, "I have the *best dad* in town!"

Had he just bought her the latest foreign sports car?

Had he given her a membership in a prestigious club?

Had he opened an unlimited checking account for her at the nearest branch of Bank of America?

She explained, "I can tell my dad anything. He's always interested in what interests me. He has time to listen, and when things have been bothering me and I talk them over with him, everything seems to get all straightened out. Every girl should have a dad like mine!"

Obviously, this desirable and hard-to-find relationship does not come about by itself. It takes years to develop such warm mutual feelings and trust. But, as long as you have that child, it's never too late to begin.

In my book, dads have a special responsibility. In a sense, we stand in the place of God to our young children. God is portrayed as a *father,* not a mother (although the mother/child relationship can never be overestimated). We teach the child to pray, "Our *Father,* which art in heaven," and the seed thought is dropped in the impressionable young mind. Also, unless at an early age they are disillusioned, children tend to be idealistic little mortals. Their concept of God is that He is good, that He is kind and compassionate (they may not know that word but they know how it makes them feel); they view Him as fair and trustworthy.

Christian psychologists tell us that it is difficult to bring a person who has never had a warm, trusting relationship with his own dad, to put his trust in God, to believe that God loves and accepts him.

The father who does not regularly and happily choose to spend time with his son or daughter is signalling loud and clear to that child, "You're not worth my time; I have more important things to do than spend my precious time playing with you or talking with you." This is discounting a vulnerable human being at a most hurting level. Some dads learn this vital lesson in the hardest of all ways, when the teenager has given up on family and on God and has turned to drugs for solace. Some learn it, tragically, too late.

Kim is the daughter of a very successful doctor who gives his life to better the lot of people in underdeveloped countries. His wife, equally dedicated, works along with him. They are carrying out Christ's commission to preach the gospel and care for the sick. Meanwhile, what is happening to young Kim and her two brothers?

Oh, their parents haven't neglected them in the usual sense of the word. Their needs for food and shelter and education have been well cared for by competent "help." And regularly for two hours on Wednesday and three on Sunday afternoon, the parents have had a special children's time. Nothing short of a major medical emergency was ever permitted to interfere with this family time. Still, recalling her childhood, Kim explained to a counselor, "It was as if Mom and Dad filed us, to be pulled out twice a week and given their total attention. The rest of the time, though, the message I got was 'Get lost; we're busy.' "

In her hurt-created bitterness, this girl became 'a behavior problem' in boarding school. She repudiated God and Christ. She flouted the moral teaching she knew, and associating with questionable characters she was soon experimenting with easy-to-obtain drugs. She was expelled from the church-related college that had accepted her because of her parents' reputation. Her whole desire was to strike back at them. "I'll get *pregnant,*" she vowed—and it was not her fault that she didn't!

No parent can afford to be guilty of child neglect, whatever form it takes. He who neglects his own household is worse than an infidel (1 Timothy 5:8).

I can't bring my daughter Diane back. But I can and will with all the strength God gives me, crusade to alert other parents. I urge you, while you still have your daughter, to ask yourself not once but often, *How well am I meeting her need to be loved, to be accepted, to feel that she belongs and is worthwhile?* Being this kind of a mother or dad is one of the surest ways I know to guard against your child's turning to drugs.

The PLEASURE
Principle

What makes drugs so tantalizing to our young people?

One clear-cut explanation is, as I see it, the general acceptance by our society of the pleasure principle. Not that pleasure per se is new to this generation. People have always sought and enjoyed pleasure. The difference in our day is the place it is given. Historically, pleasure followed and often was the reward for work well done. What is destructive in today's emphasis on pleasure is that it has no regard whatsoever for responsibility. Nor does the pleasure seeker take into account the possible dangers he risks in order to have momentary pleasure.

I think the whole American philosophy of the last fifty years has been veering more and more to the NOW. "Do it now." "Let it all hang out." "The heck with the future." The pursuit of pleasure has become a way of life for many, young and old alike.

Addressing the '79 graduating class of The Stony Brook School, Dr. Gordon MacDonald said,

> You are entering into a period of American history where it is fashionable never to say no to yourself, when it is fashionable to say yes to virtually everything. . . . Yes to the acquisition of mounting pleasure for the sheer joy of experience. And the fact of the matter is, that when people do not learn to say no to themselves in their early years, they destroy themselves spiritually. It was at this very school that I began the lesson of saying no to myself.

Any thinking person realizes that everything has its price. This is a law of God, a law of nature—"As you sow, so shall you reap"—the law of cause and effect.

But we haven't set very good examples for our kids. They've seen the parents in many instances grabbing for things to make them happy. And all too often, in our credit-card society, it's an "enjoy now, pay later" practice. And there's always one more thing to reach for, *now*. When I was growing up, people saved—more often scrimped—to obtain something they wanted. Not these days. It's instant gratification no matter what the added cost: a "why wait when we could be enjoying it today?" philosophy. And our youngsters construe this as meaning *it's OK to get what you want when you want it.*

How does this relate to the beginning of drug usage?

Someone dangles the promise of instant pleasure in the form of a joint, a sniff, a shot. And, not stopping to question, "What will it cost me? Can I afford the possible consequences?" the boy or girl succumbs to the enticement of instant gratification.

We should not be too surprised, in a way. For, as many prophetic preachers are reminding us, "In the last days [we might well be living in them] men will be lovers of pleasure, more than lovers of God" (2 Timothy 3:4). While this has always been true of a vast majority, it would seem that the whole world is on a mad whirl in search of pleasure. The Bible is awesomely accurate in its foretelling.

The Influence of Peer Pressure

Most of us would agree that this is a hard time to be growing up.

The chairman of the Los Angeles Board of Supervisors was discussing this topic with Dr. Ralph Byron, Senior Surgeon of the City of Hope, who said, "I think it's twenty times as tough to grow up now as when we were growing up."

"No," countered the L.A. official, "it's more like 100 times as tough."

Unfortunately, the latter was more accurate, as parents quickly learn (and with which Dr. Byron promptly agreed). This eminent surgeon had more to say, and with his permission I am including it here:

The sources of many of the teen problems can be summed up in two words—PEER PRESSURE.

19

There are identifiable reasons why peer pressure is a greater force in society than it formerly was for young people. Take the availability of the automobile and the motorcycle, and couple this with the magic age of 16 when the young person can drive alone. This means he or she can roam at distances which preclude parental guidance. As a boy, my range was four blocks in any direction, with home as my definite base. However, when I could drive alone, my range was 50 to 100 miles in all directions. Suddenly I found I could be with my peers alone at varying distances from my home. All at once I was exposed to the pressure of the group. And this pressure can be tremendous.

Some years ago there were the Sunset Strip Riots, teenagers rampaging through the streets of Hollywood totally out of control. An analysis of who these young people were and where they had come from revealed the following facts:

1. They represented every racial, cultural, and economic background.

2. They came from as far south as San Diego (130 miles), as far east as Nevada (260 miles), as far North as Santa Barbara (100 miles), and as far west as the Pacific Ocean (25 miles).

3. They came because they heard there would be excitement, and they strongly desired excitement. Excitement spelled pleasure for them.

4. It was possible for them to come because a couple of dollar's worth of gas, more or less, in those faroff pre-inflation days would transport them by car to where the action was.

5. They left the relative control (and safety) of home, and found themselves alone with their peers. In this setting, they did such things as they would never have dreamed of doing when alone, or at home or school.

Analyzing some of the ingredients that go into peer pressure, Dr. Byron quotes one of the great football coaches, Vince Lombardi, who said, "Nice guys always lose," then adds his own comments:

Young people have picked up this phrase and faithfully transmitted it; they have expounded it and expanded it to, "Nice guys not only lose, they never have any fun or excitement." And this suggests the corollary: if you are going to have fun, excitement, and thrills, you can't be too nice. Or—you can't belong to the group.

There is a strong desire in normal healthy young people to belong. And there's a hint—sometimes much more than a hint—that "You do what we do or you'll be left out of the group; you will be a wallflower; you won't be allowed to participate in the thrills and excitement we have."

Fear that they will be left out becomes a strong motivating force in peer pressure.

Status likewise becomes a most desirable attainment in the eyes of a young person. To gain a standing in the crowd, he must do what they do; otherwise he will be labeled as a goody-goody, and laughed at. If we will look back to our own younger days—and it's still true—people will agree to almost anything rather than be derided by the gang or lose status and equality with them.

In the crisis of decision, the young person is often pressured by several members of the group. I can speak from experience. Several years ago, I found myself in such a position. A dozen fellows were seated in a circle with me in the center. The room was locked. I was told I would not be released until I did a certain thing. The confrontation lasted for three hours before they all gave up. I learned something of what peer pressure can be.

When I was with the marines in north China, one of our surgical technicians came to me sobbing. "What's the matter?" I asked him, and he blurted out, "Dr. Byron, I went out with a gang of the fellows last night, and I did some terrible things, things I never thought I would or *could* do. I was swept along with the enthusiasm and excitement of the other guys." He tried to cover his face with his hands as he groaned, "I'm *so* ashamed." He had experienced peer pressure, and had gone down under it.

How does peer pressure fit into the drug scene?

Let me say that when I was a teenager, the drug pushers frequently looked like refugees from skid row. They were certainly not the type one would wish to emulate. But now they are more like Joe College himself, clean-cut, well-dressed. They appear and mingle at ease in a party as guests. Then, in the course of the evening the question is raised, "Have you ever tried drugs?"

History

Now

"No," you say, "I hear it's dangerous and habit-forming." Then the conversation goes like this:

"Who told you that?"

"My parents" (or "My teacher" or some other adult).

This brings the quick retort, "How do *they* know? Have they ever tried it?"

"No, but I'm sure they have good information." The pusher then goes into a stronger argument.

"The only people who get addicted are those who are weak, inadequate, unstable. Now I've tried it, and I *know* what it's like." He takes a pace back and says, "Look at me. Do *I* look like an addict! I tell you, I've taken drugs, and I know what a great experience it is. I know for myself, not from *hearsay*" (the latter with a bit of a sneer).

Two or three others, also guests at the party, chime in. "We've tried it, too. You won't really know until you try for yourself. Are you *afraid* to try? Are you chicken?"

The pressure mounts and becomes more than any but a strong personality can resist.

Unfortunately, all too often, the effect of such peer pressure is as predictable as the progression of the first Psalm: (1) "*Walking* in the counsel of the ungodly; (2) *Standing* in the way of sinners; (3) *Sitting* in the seat of the scornful."

Peer pressure is, of course, felt at other levels than that of drug persuasion. Any "in" thing results in some girls and fellows feeling,

"Everybody's got it," so I have to have it; or "Everybody's doing it," so I'd better get with it. It may be as harmless as skateboarding in a safe area or as dangerous as "chicken driving" on a busy freeway. It could be a clothes fad, or sneakers: anything that's new and that has caught on with the giant aid of TV commercials.

To the kids whose parents can't afford to provide them with the latest in everything, it can have traumatic effect. It may make sense to the parent to reason, "If that's the kind of crowd it is—if you can't be accepted unless you wear the 'uniform,' then are you sure that's the kind of friends you want?" Sensible as that line of argument is, it doesn't generally reach the kid who's dying to conform.

There's an obvious paradox; for the same kid who loudly asserts, "I don't want to be a cookie-cutter person; I want to be ME, myself—an *individual,*" is often at the same time striving with all his might to be and do and look just like the crowd he admires, the "in" bunch.

Sometimes the parents themselves go to great lengths to have their child "belong," often robbing themselves of things they need in order to provide image items for their son or daughter. Why, then, are they so confounded when the teenager emulates the group, even when it comes to drug usage or sexual promiscuity? They have projected less than true values to their child, giving him a distorted example to follow. While it's true that birds of a feather flock together, sometimes birds of another feather get the idea that it would be good to "flock" with a new group and adopt their ways.

What about the exhortation in Romans 12:2 that we should not conform to the pattern of the world? This is not "another Bible no-no" for the sake of cutting down on our pleasure. No. Like every other piece of guidance in the Bible, this is for our own good. Young people need to be helped to understand the *purpose* of Scriptural guidelines. Conforming solely for the sake of being like "everybody else," is a negative thing. (And generally, the "everybody" is really a make-your-own-rules-and-live-by-them minority.)

Conformity demeans the one who blindly follows.

Conformity causes a person to cease functioning on the basis of his own convictions and values.

Rarely are there advantages in conforming to the world's patterns. Almost always it's a retrogression. Apart from the ultimate specific effects, conforming weakens the personality and creates passive people with no minds of their own.

Sadly, kids caught up in a fad don't stop to think of the possible end results. Because this is true, *parents* need to do some thinking. It's incumbent upon us not to let our young people be snared into everything that comes along. When we suspect that they are being pressured by their peers into something that is harmful, against everything they have been taught concerning right and wrong, it is time for action. This is no time for parents to run scared of the kids. Sure, it takes guts for a mother or dad to take a stand, to be firm. And it may not make for popularity. But where have we been instructed, "Parents, be *popular* with your children"?

God has issued His mandate in both the Old and the New Testaments. We are to teach our children His ways—to be diligent about doing this (see Deuteronomy 6:7; Proverbs 22:6; Ephesians 6:4). Teaching, both by word and example, is not an elective; it is a parent's *responsibility*. It includes issuing warnings and setting limits. And we will one day be held accountable for how we have discharged this responsibility.

It's a mark of love to set limits, to say, "No, you can't do it just because everybody else is doing it." Or, as I heard Psychologist Dr. Lee Salk tell parents on a talk show, a better way is to say, "*You* don't have to do it just because the neighbors are doing it; you don't have to have it just because some of your friends have it. If the 'price of admission' is a Jaguar or a Porsche, what kind of friends are they anyway?"

Sometimes, limit-setting works when other forms of discipline do not. Susan had tried her parents' patience to the utmost. When she came home very late one night, her dad, who had been tolerant though unhappy about some of her escapades and her associates, blew up. He didn't try to disguise his anger. "Susan," he began, "your mother and I have had it. This is the last time we're going to put up with your disobedience and your insolent attitude. You know better, and I tell you we won't *have* this kind of behavior—"

He got no further. Susan cut in with, "Oh, Daddy," then she dissolved into tears. Between her sobs, she looked up, wiped her face a little, and gulped, "At last. At *last, you really care.* You care about me. I thought you and Mom didn't love me, that I didn't matter to you."

Susan's is not an isolated case.

Everyone needs attention. And we seek it by one means or another. Susan's protracted misbehavior had been her bid for attention. Fortunately, though all unwittingly, her father pushed the right button that caused her to understand she was loved.

Building up the teenager's self-esteem, his feeling of worth and belonging, is essential for good adjustment in life. The kid with even a slight feeling of inferiority or insecurity and inadequacy will look for acceptance where he thinks he can find it, not counting the cost. It doesn't take much pressure from his peers to weaken the moral fibers and spiritual values. So, especially when the young person is offered something guaranteed to make him feel like the person he admires, he is vulnerable; his resistance is low. This can lead to the first drug experience. (It needs to be said, however, that most parents really want the best for their children; they are not out to undo their children or to give them a poor start in life. Moreover, there comes a point when a young person has to take responsibility for what he is and what he is giving himself to.)

The Awesome Influence of the Entertainment World

Nowhere does the pleasure principle reach its zenith as it does in the entertainment industry. This ever-burgeoning business is more and more setting the standards in all areas of life. More people acquire their standards from movies and television than from the Holy Bible, sad to say.

How many movies portray home scenes where casual drinking is "the norm"? The husband comes home from the office and immediately heads for the home bar. Friends arrive at a party, and the host is ready with his "Can I offer you something?"—the 'something' always being equated with the contents of a bottle. Almost never does the person refuse; it would make him or her an oddball. The inference is that the normal person is a drinker. Society not only condones it; they propagate it. The message is given: This is how Mr. and Mrs. America live.

Smoking is likewise portrayed as a proper social activity.

Advertisers keep the myth going. Their well-dressed, executive-type men, and fashionable attractive women who appear with their raised glasses, endorsing Calvert's or some other brand of liquor. The setting is inviting, never an end-of-the-road miserable room; never desperate wall-climbing alcoholics who would sell their souls for one more drink; and never the patients in the emphysema ward of a hospital gasping for breath caused by lung cancer from smoking.

The brainwashing goes on. Dr. O. Quentin Hyder, New York psychiatrist, states in his book, *Shape Up* (Revell, 1979), that almost ten million Americans are either outright alcoholics or "problem drinkers" whose consumption is enough to cause serious problems both to themselves and others. Regarding smoking, he points out that nothing can be argued in defense of the filthy habit. It has absolutely no redeeming features.

It's not all drinking and smoking tobacco. There are the scenes showing young people turning on with drugs.

Do Christians escape this brainwashing input?

No. For, while many may not choose to attend the movie theater, they get the same message on the tube as the movie is allowed to pervade the living room on television. With permissiveness knowing almost no limits, everything goes on the home screen. Now with the upsurge of paid TV with its much advertised "Nothing cut, uncensored," has come another dimension diabolic in its explicit portrayal of loose morals. Some parents go off for the evening leaving their children and teenagers to view scenes which they themselves might well be too embarrassed or horrified to look at. Frequently, before the harm to the impressionable youngsters is discovered, the kids are already experimenting, implementing what they have seen on TV.

The Greater Menace

As potentially harmful as are the movies and TV, in my opinion the record industry is an even greater menace to the young mind. Also, it is more likely to go undetected.

I heard a mother gripe at the "bedlam" as her son's stereo blasted the air. In frustration she exclaimed, "That *noise.* I'm sure I don't know what my son gets out of listening to it. It's just a bunch of meaningless screaming."

She's right. She doesn't know. To her—and so many other parents—the screaming, the deafening beat, the irritating repetition is just an annoyance. If it were only the unearthly noise, it would still be harmful, for this high level decibel pollution on a day-to-day basis can't fail to have bad effects on the ears. But there's an infinitely greater danger in consistent listening to many of today's records that sell a million or more, and magnetize our young people. It's not just because of the songs themselves, their provocative titles, and the philosophy of the double-think lyrics. The greater danger is the young listeners identifying with the performers.

It's one thing to attend a movie and see glamorous stars acting out their parts. You may be attracted by their appearance or by the life-style they portray; you may have certain longings to live that way some day. But you have no association with the star. You're not going to meet him or her personally. They're living in another world, and you know it. Whatever influence the movie has on you is temporary. You return to real life when you step outside the theater. The same is not true of the rock concerts and those who frequent them. For one thing, many of the rock singers are about the same age as the kids, so they identify with them. They idolize them. Whatever these extravagantly dressed performers with their glittering instruments sing, the kids "buy" in total. They are like pied pipers. If the singer says it's cool to get high, the kids follow their philosophy.

Not all kids, or even a fraction of the "worshipers," are able to attend the rock concerts. But the recording companies take care of that. Whatever group or person is on top is heard hour after hour, day after day. So there's the repetition factor. Kids hang onto every word, every syllable. Long after the lights are out in many a home, the earphones are tuned to a radio underground station playing the latest rock songs. For the most part, parents rarely listen to the words, and if they were to, they wouldn't understand their import to the young people. To the average adult, the sound is nothing but a too-loud cacophony, a jumble of meaningless words. But the kids are getting it all. To them, the words come as from an oracle. Like the TV commercial that is repeated endlessly to sell a product, so the record industry is peddling its poison.

Do I hear some sluffing this off with, "But they're just popular songs that happen to suit today's young people. Why is so much being made of it?"

"Give me the making of the *songs* of a nation and I care not who make its *laws*." These words from the pen of Andrew Fletcher of the seventeenth century pertain today. Music has always been a potent tool for stirring the emotions. It rallies men in wartime; it provides the climate for worship; it creates the atmosphere for love. It can "soothe the savage breast," and it can bring out the animal in man.

Hit records with their hard-rock sound effects beat their rhythm all the while ploughing into young impressionable minds their sex-oriented, drug-propagating lyrics. Drugs and music have long been linked from the standpoint of reinforcing one another. I read a book about marijuana which said that jazz music in the thirties was significantly associated with this prodrug thing. And the greedy industry will latch on to anything to sell records. You may or may not know that Walt Disney, who was one of my close friends, produced a beautiful picture called *Fantasia*. This has been picked up and is being used as "drug bait." Young people flock to see *Fantasia* and become "Fantasia cultists." And they get high on LSD or PCP or another of the high drugs, not the downers. They don't necessarily intend to do such a thing; it just happens, with lights and moving images, something that complemented a cultism that came along years after Disney made the picture. So now *Fantasia* has become a cult movie. Poor Walt! If he knew, he'd be wailing over this in his grave. He was a most conservative man. He did not claim to be a strong Christian, but he believed in God, and he certainly believed very strongly in the kinds of movies and plays and amusement parks that fit in with wholesome family fun.

Nothing is sacred to money-hungry producers or the performers who wail out their noxious message. And Christians—the Christian world in general—need to face up to the fact that young people from Christian homes are not exempt. The records of counseling centers would reveal that this is so. Yet, rather than being open about it, some parents would rather sweep "the disgrace" under the rug.

Why is it that Christian faith and the company of other believers is not enough for some Christian teenagers? Why do they turn to drugs?

Again, the pleasure principle enters in.

As adamantly opposed to everything that attracts young people into the drug scene as I am, before dismissing them from society (if we could) let's learn what we can from them. Drug pushers know how to sell their product. They make converts, and all too often keep them.

More Than Entertainment

Rock music is a whole subculture; for many "disciples" of the rock heroes, it's the *real world*.

Reinforced by distinctive clothing—T-shirts and such—bizarre symbols with meaning only for the initiated, their own magazines, rock influences millions of young people, blinding them, making them non-thinking zombies.

Rock is also an industry, a most profitable industry producing the tangibles that make this subculture. All you have to do to verify just how much this industry supplies, that you would never find in our department stores, is to stray into the area of one of their widely publicized outdoor concerts.

"Weird" describes some of the popular stars. In the October '80 issue of *Teen Beat,* a star, Sylvester Stallone, known to his followers as "Rocky" is quoted as saying that he has undergone hypnosis and experienced a regression. He feels that he was once beheaded during the French Revolution! "Everytime I see a guillotine, I get a strange feeling of serenity."

And the teens blindly follow him and other rock stars with their distorted, unreal concepts as the beat goes on.

One of the currently popular labels is KISS, an innocent enough name. Rightly or wrongly I've heard this interpreted as *Knights In Satan's Service.* Certainly the grotesque face masks the group sports in performing would give credence to this interpretation of KISS.

A grandmother tells of visiting her son and being given her granddaughter's room for the duration of her visit.

The granddaughter, 15-year-old Marnie, is a record "addict." Among the strange collection of items that decorate her walls are posters of the KISS group. Said the grandmother, "I was almost afraid to wake up during the night; some of the faces glowed in the dark—and they are positively satanic. The whole room gives me an eerie feeling. I fear for my granddaughter if this is her absorbing interest at so young an age."

This grandmother's fears are well-grounded. Hopefully, she will be able to communicate them to the girl's parents and they will listen, try to get at the cause, and, as a result, be able to replace the satanic with worthwhile, normal healthy pursuits. But it won't be easy. Something has caused this teenager to give her allegiance to the rock crowd.

Parents should do everything in their power, use every bit of common sense, informed intelligence, and outside aid to help their child become a self-sufficient, stable adult. The family will always be the principal force in shaping a child's life, in building self-confidence, in establishing a set of values which will help him steer a steady course when he leaves the harbor. Nevertheless, we must be aware that we are dealing with an individual who is a part of us, but who remains unique and separate. And there are ever-increasing elements outside the family which also help shape the mind-set of today's youngster. Because of this, there is a limit to what a parent can do.

Where have Christians failed?

From my observance through the years, without being judgmental, let me say that the majority of solid, church-going professing Christians do not reflect or project what their faith has to offer. The outsider tends to view the Christian life as a gloomy scene; okay as an escape hatch from hell, but not a viable source of enjoyable living here and now.

Nothing could be farther from the truth.

The founder of our faith, the Savior Jesus Christ, made this greatest of all offers: *abundant life* (John 10:10).

If 'abundant' says anything, it speaks of a horn of plenty, good things that money can't buy, and for which all humanity yearns.

Jesus spoke much about *joy*. He told us to "ask that our *joy might be full.*" When He was leaving His disciples, His promise to them was that no man could take away the joy He was leaving with them.

What's happened to all that joy and abundant life? Did it go out with the first century? No! A thousand times no.

This joy comes from the *inside*—"a well springing up" Jesus called it. In no way can the temporary thrill or pleasure of drugs begin to approximate this kind of joy. It doesn't call for daily injections; it's always available.

Why then have so few Christians "packaged it" attractively through living joy-filled lives?

God is for pleasure as part of a normal, healthy life. The Bible speaks of "pleasures forever more" at God's right hand. And, seemingly, a lot of believers are waiting till they get to Heaven to enjoy pleasure. Meantime, we are robbing people, by our negative image, of the joys that are now. And our now generation turns away from future thinking. They want pleasure NOW.

A Christian home should be a happy place in which to live. Unfortunately, this is not always the case. The mother and dad may not be happy with each other or with their circumstances. This dissatisfaction, this lack of happiness, is easily communicated to the children. These young people will then not be too happy with themselves or each other. It's a poor recommendation for the faith of their fathers. A high-school girl complained, *"I don't know a single happy home in our church."* (It's obvious that she couldn't know all about every home in the church, but she had observed sufficient inconsistency to form her negative opinion.)

Children are not likely to reject Christianity when they are brought up in a home where love and peace and joy abound.

It's worth thinking over, in our search for solutions to the drug attraction and subsequent devastation. We may have been passing along a "Brand X" Christianity instead of reflecting the genuine thing.

Jesus himself was a veritable magnet. They couldn't keep the crowds away. He had something for everybody—little children, brawny fishermen, the learned lawyer, the despised tax gatherer, the sick, the doubter, the widow—everybody. Jesus was a joy-bringer. He broke up funerals. He enjoyed happy times with ordinary people.

True, we can't perform miracles as Jesus did. But we *can* live joyfully, and pass some joy along on our way. Happy, secure Christian young people are not too likely to go seeking for pleasure through taking drugs.

Those Insidious "ACCEPTABLE" Drugs

What is the average American child's introduction to drugs?

Oh, we wouldn't immediately categorize them as drugs. Some of them are as American as apple pie. Heading the list is aspirin. And while it has proven value, yet aspirin overdose accounts for more hospital admissions than any other drug.

Americans use more than fifty billion aspirin and aspirin compounds annually—600 million dollar's worth! 280 aspirins each on the average (U.S. Tariff Commission figure).

The manufacturer can and does make child-proof caps for the containers. He cannot supply impression-proof pills. Many children grow up regularly seeing their mother or other adults resorting to "a couple of aspirin" for the slightest twinge of pain. Seen on a consistent basis, this cannot fail to produce in the observant youngster at the least a casual attitude toward aspirin and similar within-reach panaceas. Worse, it can create the impression that this is the thing to do. And the young people grow up to reflect what they have had as an example.

Another questionable effect of seeing aspirin so freely used is this: the young person develops the concept that life should not include any form of pain, that at the first sign of an ache or pain, he should reach for a pill (perhaps later, for a drink), that will fix everything and raise his spirits. Realistically, pain is a part of everyone's life; it is one of nature's messengers—a blessing in disguise, many times, signaling that everything is not right. A headache, for instance, is often the sign that we need to relax, to reduce stress. Any physician would agree that reducing the pain of a headache through taking aspirin, without working at reducing the stress that caused it, only aggravates the problem in the long run.

It's not only aspirin. There's a whole line of "respectable drugs"—tranquilizers, diet pills, sleeping pills, etc.—which are such a part of normal living today for many people. I know some who might conceivably "leave home without their American Express card," to whom forgetting their pills would be a minor disaster. "Don't forget your pills, Mom," I heard a girl remind her mother as the mother was leaving for a few day's visit with relatives. But that same mother would have been offended, maybe incensed, had anyone called her a drug user!

What I'm saying about all this casual popping of various pills by parents and other adults is this: all unwittingly, we are giving a message to the younger generation that it's easier to take a pill than to work out a problem. Early impressions are difficult to erase. I saw somewhere a few days ago this couplet that says it all:

What a tangled web do parents weave,
Who think their children are naive.

I've spent my life with kids. I've learned something of what makes them tick. I know they have an unerring ability to sense what will make a grownup get all bent out of shape, uptight, and they will use it like a cannon. They live in a world of no-nos and fences and putdowns (from their point of view): "Quit picking your nose"; "Don't put your elbows on the table"; "Keep off the lawn"; "Don't interrupt"—

So, when they can find something that will make a grownup squirm, believe me, *they'll use it.*

As they grow a bit older, drug use is one of those things, for they well know how mortified their parents will be if they get into anything so bad. Kids have a radar for spotting double standards that is infallible, and precise to the millionth of an inch.

So we need to take a good hard look at the examples we are setting, or else be prepared for some consequences. Nevertheless, the common reaction of parents and other adults who learn that a child is on drugs is, "I can't believe it! Not my son Jim. He's always been such a good boy."

"Not that friendly kid next door. He wouldn't take drugs!"

"My granddaughter taking drugs? You can't tell me that Susie would do such a thing."

"My top English student! Surely there's some mistake. He's too smart for that."

But all of them have, indeed, fallen into the drug trap: son Jim, neighbor Pete, granddaughter Susie, and top student Andy—and they are representative of millions of others.

Are the parents of these young people indifferent and noncaring? Probably not. The majority may be average loving parents. But if we could meet and talk with them we might find a common denominator, a missing ingredient in the parent/child relationship. These fathers and mothers have gone along *assuming that everything was right with their sons and daughters*. Psychologists have a term for this. They call it "UPA"—*U*nchecked *P*rivate *A*ssumptions. To put it simply, it means functioning on the basis of something we assume to be true, without checking out the facts. Thus the incredulous, "Not *my* son," "Not *my* daughter" reaction.

The Least Suspected Drug

Tea. Coffee. Cola. Americans consume them by the millions of gallons. The caffeine they contain is a cheap, legal drug that comes from natural plant sources such as coffee beans and kola nuts. Caffeine acts as a stimulant, and affects the central nervous system.

"A *stimulant?*" I hear someone ask. "A cup of coffee a stimulant?" Yet all we need do to verify this is to be around a few people who say, "I need a pickup," and they head for the coffee pot or the vending machine. Even the church is in on this act. Seems to me that few functions get going without the inevitable "coffee time." With some visitors, I toured a church building in the Los Angeles area about an hour after the Sunday morning service. In every area of that large complex, wherever a class had been held, there was the coffee urn and the tea and the fixins, the marks of sociability.

Soft drinks containing cola are no less harmful when taken to excess. Even the innocent-looking chocolate bar, small as today's version is, contains about 25 milligrams of caffeine.

"But I *like* my coffee," we say.

Do you like it well enough to become an addict? (The drug caffeine is habit-forming.) If you doubt this, try stopping "cold turkey"; the withdrawal will result in irritability, headache, and restlessness—all signs of physical dependence.

Sometimes I hear Christian people deploring the intake of alcohol by other people while they themselves swig down countless cups of coffee. Perhaps if they were to do a little research on the harmful effect of overdrinking coffee, they might feel constrained to cut down in the interest of consistency. The Bible is clear that our bodies are "God's temples" (2 Corinthians 6:16).

Significantly, at the time of this writing, I'm hearing news items speculating as to the advisability of *placing health warning labels on tea and coffee.* Pregnant women are being especially cautioned to give these up.

We could control our own appetites without the aid of government if we would but be moderate in such things. The heavy coffee drinker could phase into decaffeinated brands which taste almost as good. The chronic tea drinker can find many varieties of tea which are not harmful to the body; the tannic acid in "regular" tea can be cut by the use of milk or cream.

The aspirin taker can find brands which do not contain caffeine. Since one of the most common causes for taking aspirin is a headache, and since excessive aspirin use is a cause of headaches, it doesn't make sense to try to cure a headache with what gives us one!

We'll all do our kids a favor if we serve them drinks that do not contain cola. A *few* cokes won't hurt them, but it's a poor habit to instill in a child. (For one thing, the sugar content is high, and we're hearing more and more of the evils of sugar in the diet.)

Top of the List

My perception of drug abuse is that the killer drug is *tobacco.* Most statistics would back this up, that on the mortality scale of deaths due to drugs, cigarette smoking tops the list. This is the drug that is both insidious and acceptable (the latter to a lesser degree, although this doesn't mean there are fewer smokers).

Smoking is something more kids try and at an earlier age than they would be likely to try other drugs. Smoking a cigarette is one of the first ways a boy will try to prove he's "old enough," that he's not scared of anybody; he'll do it to gain acceptance by the bigger boys, even if it kills him (which he feels that first smoke is going to! Nevertheless, being sick is worth it). He's feeling out his independence wings. What he's not considering is the price he will pay if he continues.

Dr. O. Quentin Hyder, a New York City psychiatrist, in his book, *Shape Up,* writes:

> Let me speak first to the teenager or young adult experimenting with cigarettes, in the hope that he will quit before he is hooked.
>
> Why do you smoke? Because you're trying to impress someone? Because your friends do it? Because a sense of security in your relationships depends on it? Because it gives you the delusion of maturity or sophistication? Perhaps because you are nervous and need a boost to your feeling of self-confidence, or, because in your anxiety you have to be doing something with your hands? Whatever your motivation, smoking is bad news. Smoking gives you a chronic, irritating, dry cough. It makes your breath stink, and your clothes reek. It gives you ugly stains on your teeth and fingers. It generally reduces the respect that mature people would otherwise have for you. It significantly reduces your physical attractiveness to nonsmoking members of the opposite sex. If you want to be physically attractive, smelling of stale smoke doesn't exactly help.

Cigarettes that char the lungs and fire up heart attacks may also smoke areas of the brain where the keys to language abilities are enclosed. This would tie into the observation of researchers in a study of children in England. Those who had smoking mothers were, by the time they reached the sixth grade, reading about one year below grade level. *(Washington Insight,* June 1979)

Coming back to Dr. Hyder:

> To the parents and other adults, let me add this: Consider the medical effects of tobacco upon yourselves. Let me give you briefly a few scary statistics.
>
> If you smoke one twenty-cigarette pack daily, you are eight times more likely to get lung cancer—twenty times more likely with two packs daily—than a nonsmoker. Upon discovery of this cancer, only 20 percent are considered operable, and of these only 30 percent— seven out of a hundred—survive five years.
>
> Smoking's most dangerous effect, statistically, however, is not on the lungs; it's on the heart and the blood vessels. Sudden death from heart attack has in some instances been found to be as much as sixteen times greater in heavy smokers than in nonsmokers. Life insurance actuarial statistics show that the average fifty-year-old who has smoked one pack daily since age twenty-one has a life expectancy eight and a half years shorter than the nonsmoker. *That works out to twenty and one-half minutes of life lost for every cigarette!*

Dr. Hyder also warns of the danger to the smoker of rising blood pressure, stroke, peptic ulcers, cancers in the mouth, tongue, lips, esophagus, larynx, kidney, and bladder. And while he gives a word of encouragement, he also states a fact of life: "If you give up smoking, almost all toxic effects will disappear within a few weeks, but *destroyed lung tissue can never be regenerated.*"

The average young person doesn't want to hear all this; he's generally turned off by "dry statistics" and red warning flags. These may even present a dare, a challenge to him to prove "it won't happen to me."

Good intentions are not enough.

You will have to find your own best way to point out to your young people the very real dangers to themselves of smoking cigarettes. I say "to themselves" because I've known cases where the parent's reason for wanting the kid not to smoke or, if he has started, to quit, is for the parents' good feelings. Christian parents, in particular, often feel that a son or daughter's smoking is a reflection on them as parents. Their "remedial" approach is something like this: "You know better than to smoke; we're a *Christian* family; how can you so disgrace us?" This is counterproductive, breathing as it does of the family's image being the important thing. Unless love and concern for the youngster who is smoking comes through loud and clear, the "warning" can tend toward even more rebellious feelings on his part. *Because the effects of smoking tobacco are so disastrous,* it will pay the concerned parent to *choose the right time, to set the climate* for listening and interacting, rather than pouncing on a boy or girl in "righteous indignation."

Here is a fact research has uncovered: girls tend to follow their mother's smoking behavior and disregard their father's. Significantly, the percentage of teenage girls who smoke is now almost as high as that of boys. Mothers, this puts the responsibility squarely on your shoulders! Even so, there's strength in unity. A mother and father *together* provide the model, for good or ill.

Alcohol and Teenagers

There has probably never been a day when social drinking was more acceptable. This is one of the insidious effects of the gradualism of our day. A practice which, not many years ago, would have called for Biblical disciplining of a church member, now goes unregarded because in some circles it is *common practice.*

What do I mean?

I have in mind the casual drinking that goes on even in Christian homes. The before dinner glass. The drink offered to a guest as a matter of course. And I'm speaking of some homes in which the Bible is read and prayer is offered before each meal.

The teenagers are included, the rationale being, "No son of mine will ever have to go to a dark, questionable bar to get his first drink. He will learn at home to take a little wine or beer. He's not then likely to be so tempted to become a hard drinker. Drink will not be 'a forbidden fruit' to challenge him." A minister hearing this line commented, "I can just see the glee in Satan's face at such talk."

It's the *first* drink—whether with parental consent or not—that leads to the next and the next. When problems develop later on, when the son or daughter becomes a victim of alcohol, it's too late to reevaluate and relive the day they offered the first drink to their child.

"Train up a child in the way he should go," the wise man of the Bible counseled (Proverbs 22:6). Note: it's not "the way he would go" or "the way you think he should go." The results are all too predictable, *"For when he is old, he will not depart from it."* So a parent needs God's guidance, and in the matter of alcoholic beverages, the apostle Paul wrote, "Be not drunk with wine, wherein is excess; but be filled with the Spirit" (Ephesians 5:18).

There is no safe level. Not everyone reacts the same to the same experience. We all know of people who can take a few drinks with no apparent effect. (I say *"apparent,"* for liquor will take its toll one way or the other.) Others, after the same intake, will show it in their behavior.

It's a clearly documented medical fact that alcohol, being extremely water-soluble, is quickly absorbed through the stomach; in seconds, it enters the blood stream, and is immediately carried to the brain. According to Dr. Hyder, "Alcohol, even in very small doses, causes blood cells to clump together, or sludge, and these can block minute capillaries, depriving local areas of the brain of vital nutrients. For reasons not yet understood, some people are apparently much more sensitive than others to this highly destructive mechanism.

The relaxed, woozy sensation the drinker experiences when the alcohol gets to the brain is actually caused by several hundred brain cells dying. These are permanently lost. *Brain cells cannot regenerate.* Even though God has endowed us with between 15 and 20 billion individual cells, the loss of thousands of them, with each drink over a period of years, eventually leads to atrophy, or actual loss of intellectual ability.

"As Shakespeare pondered (*Othello: Act II, Scene 3*)
    'O God, that men should put an enemy in their mouths to steal away their brains!' "

Your Host, the Pusher

A word about the person who takes that first drink to please his host. You see, I don't drink, so I happen to be very sensitive—maybe overly sensitive—to all my friends who say, "Oh, come on; have a drink. What's the matter?" I say, "Why should I? I don't want a drink. Why should you insist upon my having a drink in order to alleviate your conscience that you're having a drink?"

You don't have to walk into this trap; I don't.

Is the liquor industry sprouting a conscience? Or was I reading the most ironic advertisement of the century when I chanced to pick up a page of a magazine (*Time*, July 7, 1980). The background art portrayed a crashed windshield from the interior of a car. The title of the article was "Were You an Accessory to This Crime?" The implication, if you let someone drive when he has had too much to drink, you are an accessory to the crime.

Now, are you ready? The ad is signed by Seagram Distillers Company. (They add, "For reprints please write Advertising Dept. TM-780, 375 Park Ave. N.Y. 10012.")

The Coping Pills

Other "respectable" drugs are the much publicized *valium* and *librium*. These have spawned the newest class of drug addicts. I saw a figure the other day that 75% of the emergency hospital overdose victims are women from 32 to 35—some up to 45—who are on valium or librium.

These are people who are taking both drink and pills. They are frustrated, lonely, disappointed with life.

As bad as either valium or alcohol is by itself, when taken together—this is when two and two makes seven!

I've seen firsthand the effect of valium on an older person. My grandmother was, for the last three years of her life, on tranquilizers of one sort or another. Valium was one—and they would pump her full of it. She would wake us in the middle of the night in need of help. We'd call the doctor and he would say, "Give her a couple more pills." Then they would take her off valium and put her on

38

something else. When that "wouldn't work," back she went on valium. The shock to a ninety-year-old woman's system must have been horrendous. It would have been so very much better never to have started her on any such drug. But we rely upon doctors—that's their business, and we tend not to question. Let me say this for them, the medical profession is learning that tranquilizing is not the way to go; so is the pharmaceutical profession. But in our rushed, high-pressure society, drugs are still the easy way. And the patients in many instances become addicted. Such people need our help, not our criticism for "getting into drugs."

Patients to be Warned

As of September 10, 1980, the U.S. government directed pharmacists to provide patients with printed leaflets on the possible side effects of ten widely prescribed drugs. The plan, a three-year project which will then be evaluated and a decision made as to whether it will be extended to include other drugs, is to take effect in the middle of this year.

Valium, Librium, and *Darvon* are included among the ten. Others are *Tranxene, Cimetidine,* used to treat ulcers; *Clofibrate,* used in treating elevated fats in the blood; *Digoxin,* used in treating heart ailments; *Methoxalen,* used for skin pigmentation problems; *Phenytoin,* used in the control of epileptic seizures; *Thyazides,* a class of diuretic drugs used in treating high blood pressure; *Warfarin,* an anticoagulant or blood thinner that prevents blood clots.

The leaflets to be given out with the prescriptions, known as "patient package inserts" will cost about 18 cents each, and will be produced by drug manufacturers. The government will reimburse the companies for the cost of leaflets distributed with Medicare and Medicaid prescriptions.

The manufacturer of Darvon, Eli Lilly Co., already provides patient inserts. Spokesman for the firm, Russell Durbin, said, "We believe the education efforts are working" (*Los Angeles Times,* September 11, 1980).

As I travel and talk with people, the question sometimes arises, "How did *methadone* gain such respectability?"

That is a thoughtful question.

Before going into the answer, we need to think of what methadone is and does.

Methadone is a synthetic narcotic that is being used as a supportive device in the treatment of heroin addicts. It relieves the physical craving for heroin, and has a longer duration of action in the body than heroin. It thereby enables the addict to work and lead a relatively normal life without engaging in criminal activities in order to support a habit.

Since methadone is itself physically addicting, it is administered under strict governmental regulations.

The simple answer is that methadone provides a way to keep people—heroin addicts—on the job. Methadone is so powerful that it gets you up from lying around on the floor and puts you in a wheelchair so that you are ambulatory—and it keeps you there. Its effects are different from some other drugs, but it is still a seductive drug! Unless the next step is taken to get the methadone user out of that wheelchair and on his feet by cutting his drugs, he is as much a drug addict as he was when lying on the floor.

The methadone user is just less trouble, because now he's in a wheelchair; he can stay in it the rest of his life—it's a nice comfortable wheelchair.

Whose business is it?

The question is sometimes asked, "What's wrong with a person taking drugs as long as he isn't doing anyone else any harm by it?"

This is an untenable position.

No man is an island, or, as the apostle Paul put it, "None of us lives to himself" (Romans 14:7). Nowhere is this more true than in the life of a drug addict. First, the use of drugs impairs to some degree his *physical* capacities; it can affect him *mentally* and *emotionally;* it influences his *social behavior.* At best, it does not keep the promises of the good effect it will have on its victim. At worst, it can be responsible for his death. That's the addict himself.

What of the family heartache, the shattered hopes and dreams of parents for sons and daughters?

What of the loss to the world or potential wrapped up in the person who has turned to drugs?

What of the image of God in the person?

No one can harm himself, whether through drugs or some other means, without its affecting those around him who care for him.

The drug addict in many instances becomes a drain on society as he, increasingly, is unable to function well enough to earn a living.

One person's habits influence others, especially if the person is well-known or much admired.

An Unfair Deal

Without question in my mind, the greatest evil is when a pregnant woman becomes dependent on drugs and inoculates her unborn child. This is called "the fetal alcohol (or other drug) syndrome." Recently there have been television shots of a newborn infant in the throes of drug withdrawal, surely the cruelest of all legacies to give a child just coming into the world. This should shock us right to the core if we have any spark of humanity in us. Innocent babies—victims of drug abuse.

Then, what of the child growing up in a family in which one or both parents are into drugs—and there's plenty of that these days. Probably the child was born with some of the same propensity, we don't know for sure. Science is divided—the jury is still out—on the question of how much a part heredity and genetics play in the child's bent toward drug usage. But there is no question as to those who are born addicted!

Whose business is it?

As long as innocent people, whatever their ages, are being victimized by another's drug habit, it had better be *somebody's* business.

The user himself is not going to be able to deal with the harm he may be doing; he needs help himself.

Whose business is it?

It's *our* business—yours and mine. It's up to us to take every step, to move in every direction, to push open doors, to awaken the conscience of those who are indifferent to this great evil in our midst.

We *are* our brothers' keepers.

Drugs and the
TEN COMMANDMENTS

Why did God issue the ten all-time "Thou shalt nots"? So that He could keep from fretting in His Heaven over the failure of His highest creation?

Certainly not! The Commandments were given for man's own good.

Envision, if you can, a world in which the Ten Commandments are all kept? There would be no murder, no stealing, no adultery, no lying, no coveting. Everybody would be worshiping, honoring and obeying God and dealing righteously with his fellowman. I'll leave it to the statisticians to figure on their computers the economic ramifications. But what of the moral, spiritual, physical, and psychological areas of man's life? And what do the Ten Commandments have to do with one's use of harmful drugs?

Plenty. How can we love God and deliberately violate the self that is made in His image, as every drug abuser does? It is impossible to honor our Creator while dishonoring His workmanship. Further, Christ emphasized thou shall love thy neighbor as thyself. Ah, that last little phrase, "as thyself." Now there's something to ponder! For too long, its impact has been hidden; rarely, until the past few years, have I heard a preacher spell out the implications of loving myself.

What if I don't love myself? What if nothing in my background or environment has ever contributed to my loving—or even liking myself? What if I have never felt worthwhile or important or accepted, so that I have never accepted myself?

Failure to obey the laws of God results in the devastation of society at large. Failure to love oneself in the healthy sense of the word results in deep emotional problems. And turning to drugs is, all too frequently, the dire effect.

I want to share with you something from the pen of Dr. Clyde M. Narramore, one of today's outstanding Christian psychologists.

Preventing and Solving the Drug Problem

Need I remind any wide-awake parent these days that the problem of drug use and abuse has reached its tentacles into all classes of our society? It has jumped economic and social barriers, and now thousands of young people from even Christian homes and evangelical churches are experimenting with various drugs. Tragically, many of these youngsters are already hooked.

Why are drugs so enticing?

Why, in the face of overwhelming evidence of the irreversible damage these produce, do young persons continue to be drawn into the clutches of this habit? One explanation is as old as Eve in the Garden of Eden: *curiosity*. People are inquisitive beings at heart. They want to try things, to see for themselves, often not taking the consequences into account.

"Get a new feeling"; "Get smart"; "Join the in crowd": such are the titillating motivations for experimenting with new things. Perhaps one of the most intriguing allurements of drugs is this: "Expand your mind." Since the dawn of history, man has longed to be smarter, to know more; in short, to unleash his full mental capacity. A trip on drugs, many believe, may bring this about.

"Of course I won't go too far," they assure themselves and each other. "I'm just experimenting. I'll stop before the practice can harm me." But all too often, the innocent and naive experimenter ends up as a hopeless addict—or a *statistic*.

In my profession we have a saying, "All behavior is caused." What, then, beyond experimentation are the causes of drug abuse?

Many voices are being heard.

"Our young people need a different community environment," says the *sociologist*.

Psychologists state, "These are emotionally disturbed young people. They come from disrupted, emotionally deprived homes."

Law enforcement agencies agree that "The laws are too lax; punishment is not severe enough. We need to bear down on these young drug abusers."

Parents are blaming the schools, while the *school authorities* are complaining, "What can you expect? Think of these kids' homes!"

After years of studying the problem and counseling with boys and girls and teenagers, I want to submit some findings born of experience and of deep concern and conviction.

First, while the drug abuse is a serious matter, *it is a symptom* rather than the heart of the problem.

Parents, by the scores, come to our counseling centers or write or phone me frantically telling me, "My son (or my daughter) is on drugs!" As I listen and talk with them I find that their major concern is not the causes of this unacceptable behavior but rather the symptoms. They are tense and uneasy to the point of being incoherent that this thing has happened in *their* family, with *their* child. They are understandably embarrassed about the child's running away from home, or being apprehended by the authorities. Rarely, however, do I hear parents speculate, "I wonder what our son is trying to tell us; what is causing him to behave in this way? What is he really after?" No. The parents' attention is almost always on how to get the kid back home and make him behave—the symptoms.

Naturally, we cannot close our eyes to the fact that our child is in jail, or lying in a drugged stupor somewhere while "expanding his mind." Our greater concern, however, ought to be for him as a person—his motivations, the reasons why he is doing what he is doing. Unless we concentrate on the causes, we are doing only a little patch job instead of giving lasting help. Parents should be attacking the cause: the lack of certain ingredients that must go into a human being to make him become a well-adjusted person.

The Horizontal Relationship

Everyone, as he is growing up, needs solid, horizontal relationships. That is, meaningful, satisfying involvements with human beings, a warm desirable, give-and-take relationship with those who are nearest to him. This means parents, teachers, friends. Of course the parents are the core people.

From the day a child is born until he is an adult, his greatest need is for parents who want him, who protect him, who care for him, who show love and affection toward him, who trust him and are interested in him and in what he is doing; parents with whom he has good times just talking and planning and laughing. In other words, children need quantities of old-fashioned love from fathers and mothers. Not over-indulgent love, but expressions of affection that spring from a happy, well-adjusted parent.

How often such love is missing. Take Dick, for example. Ever since childhood, he has been made to feel that he doesn't quite measure up. He can "never do things right" in the eyes of his parents. So they hassle him all the time. No matter that their nagging stems from their concern and their desire to see him achieve. It's a kind of love. But what a gnarled, twisted way to love a son or daughter!

Then there's Mary. She has grown up with only one parent most of her life. She feels guilty that she is worthy of only one parent while most of her friends have both father and mother. And she feels ashamed deep down. Even worse is the fact that she is going through childhood and early adolescence deprived of the comfort and satisfaction of spending happy times with both parents. This is one of the most important and richest experiences of life. And, sadly, the film of childhood cannot ever be run through the second time. So Mary grows up with unhealthy feelings, feelings which she cannot explain even to herself. She just knows she "feels bad."

Not only the parent, but the school teacher or Sunday-school teacher can have an adverse effect on a growing child. This can be done by being over-critical, through failure to meet his emotional needs for feelings of worthiness, success, and security. I remember a dope peddler named Steve. Years before he got into drugs, he had great difficulty in learning to read even though he was a bright, handsome lad. Unknown to his parents, or Steve himself, he had a neurological impairment (degree of brain damage) which impeded his reading. His Sunday-school teacher, with distorted "good intentions" would regularly make fun of him: "What's the matter with you, Steve? A big eleven-year-old and you can't read! Aren't they teaching reading in the public school any more?" And the others in the class would titter. This went on Sunday after Sunday until finally Steve was big enough to stalk out of his home, leave Sunday school for the last time, find a gang, and start smoking pot. In this gang, he had acceptance if nothing else. The kids liked him just as he was, and they let him know it. A basic emotional need was being met. Finally, he became a pusher, all unknown to his folks. Imagine their feelings—and the surprise of the Sunday-school teacher—when they learned that Steve, now 16 years of age, had been picked up and taken to juvenile court.

A few days ago, I listened to a young fellow as he told me, "Dr. Narramore, in all my life I can't recall that I've ever had one real conversation with my own Dad." And, as events proved, if ever a fellow needed the right kind of father, it was this boy! His dad is a successful businessman, financially prosperous, yet he has, knowingly or not, robbed his own son of those things which money cannot buy. Reminds me of something I read recently: *What shall it profit a man if he gain the whole world and lose his own son?* This man bosses his son and daughter around, crabs at them all the time, and finds fault with them continually. Meanwhile, he and his wife rub shoulders with prominent people, and live it up. But at home, the father neglects to spend happy times with his own teenage youngsters. They are poles apart. In this situation, there is going to have to be a radical change in the father's personality before there will be any change in his attitude toward his son who realizes how deprived he is of fatherly caring.

Saying to this man, "Now you, sir, are going to have to make a change; you'll have to become a different person," will in no way accomplish this change. Attitudes are difficult to alter.

How does the desired change take place?

First, this father should see a professional counselor who will help him to face up to himself, and aid him in effecting the changes in his life. Further, he needs to totally commit his life to God. The change will not be easy. It will be a struggle, but the Lord will be with him. The resultant satisfactory relationship between the father and his son will change and influence both of them for the rest of their lives. I have seen such transformations when the man was ready to admit to his need to change. Is the price worth the result? I'll let you answer.

Another near tragedy just came to my attention. Here was a family who had virtually lost their oldest daughter. She had run away from home, and had been caught with drugs in her possession. Her parents were frantic and bewildered as to what to do. The authorities released the girl to her parents' custody. Stormy sessions ensued among the three of them. At their wits' end, the parents sought out a professional counselor. After all the tests and initial counseling session, the psychologist recommended something which appeared radical to the parents.

"I needn't tell you," he said, "that you have as good as lost your girl. Unless you can somehow bridge this gulf that's separating you, she will run away again. She'll probably become an addict *and she may never come back home.*" He watched as they digested his warning and reacted with looks of combined terror and unbelief, then he continued, "Now you're not going to want to do what I'm asking you to do. It may be bitter medicine, I realize. But as I see it, this is the only possibility of holding your daughter. Here's what you must do:

1. Treat her like an adult even though she's not always responsible and seemingly worthy of such treatment.

2. Let her do at least half the talking without your interrupting and challenging everything she tries to say.

3. Ask her what *she* would like to do; let her express her opinion.

4. Don't *force* her to go to Sunday school or church. Your insistence might just backfire.

In time, if you will be patient and try out these suggestions, you might possibly develop a new, good relationship with your daughter."

Nothing else had worked in this case—and the parents realized they had a daughter to lose. This was a full-blown emergency, and it called for emergency measures. So they followed the counselor's advice. There were times, to be sure, when their patience was sorely tried, and ran out. They found themselves issuing the same edicts that had earlier sparked the girl's rebellion: "You *will* do this," or "You *can't* do that; we won't *permit* it," and the girl's defiance flared up. At times, she deliberately took advantage of them and the situation she had brought on them. But gradually, there came an easing of the tension between them, a degree of understanding of each other, a willingness to bend in each other's direction at least. The father learned to say, "I'm sorry," and his daughter's, "Oh, that's all right,

Dad; I make mistakes too," began to cement a bond between them.

Now I do not by any means want to leave you with the impression that I believe permissiveness to be the great solution. I don't! But when you've been doing the wrong thing for 15 or 18 years, and a crisis has developed between you and your son or daughter, this calls for extreme measures. If a father and mother have never fostered a desirable give-and-take, happy relationship with their children, they can't suddenly develop this when they find that their child is on drugs. It is difficult indeed to change an adult. But any one of us, regardless of age, as long as we are alive and breathing *can* change, even though it may take months of professional guidance, and many a disappointment along the road. But it will be worth it all.

The Alternative

When a child's needs are not met—when the proper ingredients are consistently missing—he will go to all extremes seeking these horizontal relationships. So when he joins the crowd who are experimenting with drugs, he identifies with them as he too becomes involved in drug usage.

These young people, on a quest for identity "find themselves." They are accepted. This represents to them the great beginning of their search for relatedness; feeling close to others. Unwholesome and dangerous as it is, they have finally begun to establish horizontal relationships.

The Vertical Relationship

Another important relationship for which boys and girls and teenagers—all human beings—are seeking is a vertical relationship, a relationship with God. Oh, I know people are not saying this out loud, they're not sporting lapel buttons that read, "Help me find God"; but the yearning is there, as so well expressed by St. Augustine: "Thou has made us for Thyself, and our hearts are restless until we find our rest in Thee."

This dissatisfaction with themselves, this inner restlessness, is a vital, driving force that relentlessly entices thousands of our young people to seek satisfaction in the mirage of drug use and abuse.

The question comes to me so frequently, "I can understand kids from unhappy or broken homes, where there may be no Christian teaching, reaching out for drugs. But what about the many who go to church and Sunday school, who have Christian parents yet who are caught in this dope net?"

Well, they might have good Bible instruction, and live in a "Christian atmosphere," but still not have loving, caring parents who meet their needs. Or, it may be that although they are attending church and Sunday school, it has little or no meaning for them; it has not influenced their values and priorities. Their head knowledge has not reached their heart, affecting their behavior and choice of companions.

Too many parents expect their children to act like Christians before they are Christians. They may sing the hymns and be able to quote some Bible verses and even know how to pray. But that's not enough. They need to experience a satisfactory relationship with God through accepting His Son Jesus Christ; they need to be born again.

This relationship with God cannot be fully described. As a Scottish woman expressed it, "It's better felt than telt(told)"; it's wonderful! Not that it must be an emotional experience. Very often it is not. But it must be real. And the Holy Spirit who lives within guides the believer into clean living, clean speaking, clean motives, and clean relationships. We are accepted, we are secure through Christ, we can feel worthwhile, and all our emotional needs for belonging and feeling loved and worthy are fully met, regardless of the deprivation of one's childhood years.

A satisfying horizontal relationship with people and a meaning-filled vertical relationship with God: these two, when realized, are both a preventative and a solution to the problem of drug usage.

You may obtain a copy of the above material in booklet form by writing The Narramore Christian Foundation, Box 5000, Rosemead, CA 91770. Ask for Booklet #68.

As for "loving our neighbor," this commandment is violated day after day by the drug addict driven to stealing by the need to support his habit. As never before in history, people are unsafe on the street, in their homes, strolling in a park. Innocent victims are mugged, sometimes for a few dollars or less. Once hooked, the drug user is a virtual slave to his craving. Nothing matters—God's laws or man-made ones—nothing but that joint, that pill which will satisfy the demon, or blot out the problems of the day.

I heard of an old farmer who was at the end of his patience with school children stealing from his orchard. He had posted "No trespassing" signs, had added "Trespassers will be prosecuted" and a few other prohibitions. Nothing had scared off the kids. At last, in desperation, he posted a huge sign, THOU SHALT NOT STEAL. That did the trick. Where man's warning hadn't made a dent on the kids' conscience, God's Word was effective. I'm not so sure even this would work with the desperate drug abuser. Nevertheless, I do know of instances where, when all other methods and people had failed, the Word of God in the hands of an understanding, compassionate, dedicated, caring Christian has worked wonders.

Christian parents confronted with the knowledge that their child is on drugs would do well to blend their emphasis on God's laws with a generous portion of compassion and understanding.

DRUG ADDICTION—
Where Did It All Start?

No. California didn't start it all. But the grim statistics are that marijuana has just taken over as California's number one cash crop.

Drugs have always been with us. From earliest history, people could be helped or hurt by the herbs and weeds known for their potency on the human body.

Not always have these been headline news. Not always have they engaged the attention of law enforcement agencies, school authorities, and other social groups. Or parents.

The pattern has been that there is a rise in drug use and abuse following any revolution, any cataclysmic social upheaval. Such things precipitate a flight to some kind of escape: drugs, booze, or both.

The Civil War brought with it the invention of the hypodermic needle, and the use of morphine. In its wake came a tremendous drug problem in the United States with what was called "the soldiers' drug" (morphine). Its effects were so extreme that a cure was sought. Then along came the Bayer Aspirin Company with their solution to the problem of morphine addiction. This appeared to be such a miracle that it was given the Greek name, *Hero*. Hence *heroin*, which they believed to be good. They really thought it would be the cure for morphine! Years later—in the fifties—another new drug was introduced, a "cure" for heroin addiction, the much discussed and debated drug methadone. Methadone is in many ways worse than heroin. So we see the historical progression of the use of drugs.

If we go back far enough, we see that the drug scene was first of all medicinal, then it became a religious-heightening experience. Next, it became addictive either psychologically or physically. Many people do not realize that addiction is as much psychological as it is physical. In this connection, we need to consider another aspect of drug usage.

The Addictive Personality

The question is frequently asked, "Is there such a thing as an addictive personality?"

The experts tell us there is. And they pinpoint certain identifiable traits of the person who is likely to become involved with drugs more than others in like circumstances.

- *A low frustration tolerance;* they are short-fuse persons.
- *Excessive dependency;* they have great needs.
- They are *impulsive and immature* in decisions and actions.
- They're plagued with *feelings of personal inadequacy:* ("*I* can't do it," regardless of whether this is true or not).

Some addicts are sociopathic. They have character flaws that enable them to defy society with no resulting qualms of conscience; they have no thought of the consequences to themselves or those around them. Quick self-gratification is their goal, no matter who has to pay for it. Some of these are respected church members; they're just living by rules they make themselves—*rules which seem right to them.*

The mind of this kind of youth has a different filter. He tends to be a great con-man and deceiver. He can really fool his parents and family. It's believed that, for such a personality, drugs just modify what is already there.

No Place for Smug Attitudes

Few American teenagers or even younger children are completely safe from all exposure to drugs. As a parent, you may have done all the right things with and for your children, including inculcating into them Bible principles and precepts. They may be genuine Christians—"the last persons who would ever be tempted to take drugs." Don't be too sure. The statistics do not bear this out.

The danger is all the more real because the evidence is that generally it's one of their own group, not a pusher, who introduces the nonuser to marijuana.

Nor should you take comfort in checking the drug personality and seeing that your child doesn't fit into any of the descriptions. Those who have studied drug addiction have found that *any person*—whatever the personality type—*if he regularly for a few weeks uses drugs*—*can develop a dependency,* become an addict.

Those who make money from marketing drugs are no respecters of age, or sex, or color, or religion, or economic status; and they don't care whether or not your child has "a drug personality."

Who is an addict?

Narcotics Anonymous would say the addict is one whose entire life and thinking centers in drugs in one form or another, the getting and using and finding ways and means to obtain more. One who uses drugs to live—and who lives to use drugs.

The Narcotics Anonymous Program

N.A. is a fellowship of recovered addicts who meet regularly to help others to whom drugs have become a major problem. They have only one requirement for membership: the honest desire to stop using.

There are no MUSTS, but they suggest the newcomer keep an open mind, and give himself a break.

The program is a no-strings-attached set of principles written so simply that anyone can follow them in daily life. The most important thing is that THEY WORK. The group's history shows that those who keep coming regularly stay clean.

How It Works

These twelve suggestions are the principles that made our recovery possible.

1. Admitting that we were powerless over our addiction, that our lives had become unmanageable.

2. The belief that a power greater than ourselves could restore us to sanity.

3. The decision to turn our will and our lives over to the care of God.

4. Making a searching and fearless moral inventory of ourselves.

5. Admitting to God, to ourselves, and to another person the exact nature of our wrongs.

6. An entire readiness to have God remove all these defects of character.

7. Humbly requesting Him to remove our shortcomings.

8. Making a list of everyone we had harmed, and becoming willing to make amends to them all.

9. Following through and making amends wherever possible except when to do so would injure them or others involved.

10. Continuing to take personal inventory, and when wrong, admitting it promptly.

11. Praying for God's will for us, and the power to carry it out.

12. Having had a spiritual awakening as a result of these steps, we tried to carry the message to addicts, and to practice these principles in all our affairs.

This sounds like a big order, and we can't do it all at once; we didn't become addicts in one day. So remember, easy does it.

One thing that will defeat the addict in his recovery, more than anything else, is an attitude of indifference or intolerance toward spiritual principles. Although there are no MUSTS in N.A., there are three indispensable attitudes: Honesty, Openmindedness, and Willingness to try. *(This information is courtesy of Narcotics Anonymous, P.O. Box 622, Sun Valley, CA 91352. More complete information available upon request.)*

Dr. Quentin Hyder would add his endorsement to the spiritual emphasis expressed by the N.A.

Our bodies cannot be effective vehicles for expressing the Spirit within if we fool around with them as though they were experimental laboratories. It is not possible to "glorify God in your body" if that body is not physically and mentally in first-class working order. . . . Also, since God himself is the ultimate reality, the Christian's personal relationship with God is his ultimate source of joy. The pot smoker is trying to escape from reality by obtaining his artificial "high." The Christian, by contrast, finds his high by relating to reality and doing God's will in the real world. Jesus is the best high. The joy of relating to Him cannot be remotely duplicated by temporary trips into euphoria, illusion, excitement, exaggerated sensations, erotic stimulation, or altered perceptions.

The often-heard claims that marijuana heightens one's sense of reality and deepens insights are purely subjective experiences. The high mood and insight cannot be shared with others, and the fact is that objective creativity ability is not as has been said—increased. The drug experience does not lead to anything of value beyond itself. It is narcissistic pleasure for its own sake, not capable of leading to any lasting achievements.

What if drugs were to go away?

Drugs are here to stay; they are not going to go away. For some people, that would seem the solution to the whole problem.

But would you want that to happen? Would you want to rob the medical profession of a means whereby suffering can be alleviated? Do you want to revert to the days of operations without benefit of anaesthetics? Would you want to see victims of cancer and other dread diseases go on in intolerable pain?

I think not.

The point at issue is the *control of drugs* so that they are in the hands of the right people.

It was not the legitimate use of drugs that set me off on my lifelong crusade. It was the evil of dope too easily obtained by youngsters who use it to their own harm.

We need to keep a balanced perspective. Oh, it's not easy when it's your kid who is smoking or sniffing or shooting poison into his flesh. How well I know! I wanted to lash out in every direction against everything to do with drugs. But I learned after a while not to throw out the baby with the bath water.

By indiscriminate haranguing against the use of all drugs, we just weaken our case, and make ourselves appear foolish, uninformed vigilantes. This helps nobody.

Our ammunition needs to be aimed at the illegal traffickers: the dealers, the pushers, the songs, and the magazines such as *High Times, Daily Dope,* and *Stone Age,* which make drugs so attractive to our young people—at *anything* that will snare even one child.

Beyond Prevention

It's vital that we take preventive measures. But we must not stop there. We must use our powers to get help for those who are already addicted.

There is no single way, no one-step easy solution. Don't hand me that stuff about *the* reason a kid turns to drugs. There's no *one* reason. The people who would say there is just one reason follow up with, "Therefore there is *one* solution." Deliver me from such dogmatic oversimplification. I know people too well for that!

So what can we do? Where do we start?

Fortunately, in many areas, concerned people have already instituted programs that are working.

Every community needs at least three things:

A hot line—manned by persons who not only are informed about drugs, but (perhaps more importantly if a choice has to be made) persons who are compassionate, and who have a more than usual understanding of young people and their problems. The ability to listen is a prime requisite. There are many kinds of listening; what I mean is the listener who works at it so that he can get a clear message from the person at the other end of the line, not choking the channel by his rush to give his viewpoint without giving the person a chance to really explain. The conversation won't always be coherent; it won't always make sense to the listener. But to the caller, it can represent someone who cares enough to let him talk—and he may never have had anybody like that before.

This can be a tremendous ministry for the church; Christians have the answers to life's great questions. But the personnel must be chosen not for their zeal and willingness alone, but for their suitability. A condemning, judgmental attitude can undo in a minute what other Christians may have been striving for weeks to build up.

A Crisis Center is another "must" if the young users are to be helped. Ideally, it will be a 24-hour, seven-days-a-week facility (crises don't have "hours" in which they happen). And again, the director and support personnel need to be qualified to meet the crisis.

I'd like to see communities provide *hospital beds especially for the treatment of people with drug problems.* And it would help immeasurably if they were under the care of doctors and nurses with specialized training. (We could do a lot worse with some of the funding provided hospitals.) For it has been proven that *the right treatment under the right circumstances does work.*

Why Logical, Sensible Efforts Fail

Some time ago, I was interviewed by a Canadian journalist, Milan Korcok. Among other areas, he was interested in why education has not been enough to make kids shy away from drugs. He asked me to assess the factors.

I had to agree with him as to the ineffectiveness of the programs. I told him that we on the coordinating council saw the project as a flop, that 60% to 80% of the money spent on drug education had been wasted. Why? Because we rushed into educational programs on a crash basis. We meant well. We were in a hurry, for it was—and is—an emergency. We didn't evaluate the programs before they were put into effect, they were not evaluated after, and in many cases they have proven to be counterproductive.

In too many instances, we were teaching kids to use drugs by bringing it to their attention in a dramatic fashion, exciting their interest and sense of adventure. By trying to scare kids, we have made drugs dramatic and interesting.

It seemed we were doing the rational, sensible thing, and because our method failed, some people out of frustration and anger, saw only one alternative—to jail them.

Now, years later, I realize that you cannot just trust an adolescent or teenager with the facts and then let him make the judgments. Also, I learned early in this business that there are no generalities. There is no exclusivity. The drug problem is as diverse as every human being, and every human being is unique.

From what I've seen of the educational process, the kids in grammar school and elementary school and even junior high are usually trusting, idealistic kids. You could take one of them and put him through the whole cycle of drug knowledge and reinforcement, boy scouts, athletics—all the constructive forces—and he's just great. Suddenly he turns 13 or 14, and this wonderful kid can flip over so fast it's frightening. What has happened? He's come up against the adolescent maelstrom—girls, his body maturing, peer pressure, the need to be sophisticated before his time, thrill seeking, chance-taking.

We thought that if we could start right out in the first grade and identify drugs nonemotionally as a no-no, then we wouldn't have to worry. Kids would catch on as they did to being careful crossing the street and being careful with matches. They would be safe because we had taught them. But they're not safe, because drugs have many, many overtones that these other things do not have.

There is much we can do in this era. It will take concerted effort on the part of parents, social agencies, law enforcement agencies, and the church. May it not be that the church of Jesus Christ will drag its heels years behind the others. Christians should be in the very forefront: informed, with defined goals and untiring enthusiasm. Our children and teenagers are worth it!

That First, Crucial Reaction

Parents are often the last to find out that their child is "doing drugs"; they learn from a neighbor, from one of the others in their own family, or some other way. No kid is going to come and say outright, "I'm taking drugs; I need your help." (In retrospect, my wife and I know that Diane, by some of the things she said and did, was making a bid for help. She knew she was in trouble. But we did not.)

The normal first response is unbelief. Carol Burnett has said that when she first suspected her daughter, Carrie, might be taking dope, she wouldn't let herself believe it. She resorted to snooping in her daughter's room, not in the hope of finding some evidence, but hoping she would not find any signs that Carrie was smoking pot or was otherwise involved in drugs. She didn't want to have her suspicions confirmed.

It's how the parent(s) react at this point that can often determine what will become of the young drug user.

A couple, Angela and Bill, learned that their 15-year-old Paul was smoking marijuana. What did they do? They hit the ceiling. Screamed at each other. Blamed each other. "It's all your fault, Bill," Angela accused. "You're never home; the boy never sees you."

Bill retorted, "And what about you? Are you the model mother? How nice and pleasant are *you* when Paul asks if he can have some of the guys over? Do you cooperate? Oh, *no!* The fellows might get some spots on your precious carpet, mess up the house a bit—" And so it went, for it's a well-known fact that a crisis often brings to the boil something that has been simmering for a long time.

If the parents' reaction to each other was a storm, when Paul came home, he was greeted by a full-blown tornado.

He had hardly gotten in the door when his dad thundered, "How dare you disgrace your mother and father by such behavior! Oh, we know all about you and the marijuana. Whatever will the church people think, what will they say when they learn about this?"

His mother added her tirade, "A boy with a good home like you have, and all we try to do for you! Is this how you repay us?"

Paul stood, scuffing first one foot then the other on the kitchen floor. He glanced from his mother's face to his dad's, then said in a hopeless kind of voice, "You wouldn't understand," and he headed for his room.

Predictably, the gulf will widen between this lad and his parents. They will likely maintain their, "How could you do this to us?" stance; their son will no doubt seek means to deaden his feelings of emptiness, and be all the more drawn to the friends who won't be shocked by his behavior, who don't care about rugs and things, and who understand.

Let me be quick to state that I'm not taking pot shots at Christian parents per se; this couple would have been the same—maybe worse—if they had not been church members. It's all the more disillusioning, though, to find people who follow the kind, compassionate Christ, and yet show little of His spirit toward their own son.

By contrast, I heard a heartwarming story of a Christian couple and their dealings with their daughter who was picked up by the authorities for being on dope. "She's your problem," the officer told the father when the girl was released into her parents' custody.

"Oh, no, she isn't," the father protested. "She's not my problem; *she is my daughter,*" and he gathered her tenderly into his arms. He and his wife sought professional help for her, and while not condoning her recent behavior, they supported her all through the therapy sessions. The outcome? She is clean and free from drugs; she and her parents have a warmer relationship than ever. Reinforced by their expressed and demonstrated love plus the teaching of the Bible and her friendships with other Christian young people, she is not a likely candidate for future trouble with drugs.

But I do not want to draw comparisons between parents. There's too much beating parents over the head these days. All too many are falling for the line, "You have the problems you have because your parents have failed in this or that way." (The late Joe Pyne, talk-show host, once defined psychology as, "Lying on a couch, squealing on your mother.")

The truth is that most of us want to bring our children up right. But we fall short, I think, in not keeping our eyes and ears open to the changes in the society into which our kids are hurled as teenagers. We're so busy with the demands of each day as it comes, that we don't take time to stop and analyze and evaluate what's really going on.

Gone is the day when a youngster came home from school and

there was Mom. With a cookie in one hand and a glass of milk in the other, he could spill out to her what his day had been like. They didn't call it *communication,* but that's what it was, the most satisfactory kind of communication.

Not every home was, of course, a Norman Rockwell ideal. But, by and large, family members had more time for one another than we do now. And we had fewer neurotics than today's society is spawning.

Another thing that's working is good, old-fashioned work. We can't live in a vacuum—time has to be consumed—and the time that used to be taken up with chores and regular daily duties of one kind and another sometimes hangs heavy on a modern teenager's day. This idleness can set him off looking for meaning of some kind.

Work also makes a person tired, and bed looks good after hours of heavy work, before and after school. So there was not so much gadding about in search of a good time night after night.

A job well done—no matter how we might rather have been doing something else—brings good feelings of accomplishment. It creates a sense of worth. Many of our kids have never had that feeling; they haven't felt needed or useful for anything. In an effort to "give them what we never had "—namely, pleasures and freedom from the grind of work—we may well have been robbing them.

What I'm saying is this: our young people, many of them, are suffering from feelings of "Who needs me? What am I good for?" Sadly, in drugs they find something that makes them feel different about themselves.

I don't want to be a stuck whistle, wailing about on the subject of drugs. But somebody has to sound the alarm. As I stated to the United Nations Assembly back in 1971, "Drug abuse is human misery compounded by human misunderstanding. My personal and professional energies are yours . . . to use in this work."

This is still my determination.

There has always been a search for escape from anxiety. For many, it has long been the drug routes. The difference now is that, while this escape into drugs was once confined pretty much to the upper classes, it's common to all classes. The fact is that *fewer than 1% of Americans take no forms of drugs.*

What we need to do—what we've got to do if we would see changes—is get at the bloodstream of this society, and purify it.

Surely this is the business of the church and her people!

FAMILY
Contributors

Distraught parents, horrified to learn that their Jack or Judy is on drugs, sometimes confine to the home their looking for reasons. Yet, there are often subtle reasons why a son or daughter will turn to behavior that is totally out of character with everything the home stands for.

What are some of these factors that can at least partially explain this departure from what has been taught at home?

Competitiveness

Mark is a brain. Getting all A's is a breeze for him. But in his heart, he really doesn't want to excel in the head department. Why? His brother Phil is a star athlete. And sports is what his folks are interested in. With all his academic achievements, Mark can't make it with his mom and dad, as his brother does.

In an attempt to get in on some of the attention Phil regularly got at home, Mark tried out for football. He failed dismally, and he didn't fit in. About that time, he met some fellows who were into the drug scene. They welcomed him into their circle, rather intrigued that the class brain was interested in looking their way. They accepted him as he was; he didn't have to prove himself to be accepted. He didn't want the brainy crowd. The sports crowd didn't want him; and, as he interpreted it, his parents didn't want him either. He couldn't bring them the kind of "glory" his brother did. So he latched onto the people who satisfied his need to belong.

Jill's case is similar. The younger daughter in a Christian home where love didn't seem to be missing, she felt unaccepted by her parents. Her sister was the model daughter. Her grades were always good. Teachers and school principals always spoke highly of her. She was always making her parents proud of her.

Meanwhile, Jill could never match her sister's performance. She tried, but good grades came hard for her; playing the piano beautifully seemed beyond her. Socially, she felt miserable although she desperately wanted to be popular like Anne, her sister. Then she fell in with a group who introduced her to the "joys" of smoking pot. They let her be one of them.

These two, Mark and Jill (not their real names) are among thousands of kids who have the same need for acceptance.

"Why are they rebelling?" the parents ask.

They are not necessarily rebelling, although some are. In Jill and Mark's case, it wasn't rebellion per se; it was a bid to satisfy a normal, universal hunger. Everybody longs to be accepted, not everyone is willing to face the consequences or reckon on the price.

Where the family contributes is in not recognizing the child's need, not watching the signals till it's too late.

The Right to Be Different

Parents will do well to be sure they do not require one child to be like another.

"I got sick of hearing Dad say, 'Brad, why can't you be like your brother? Why do you always have to be different?' " Earl griped.

The "different" may be in clothes, hairstyle, choice of recreation, any one of a dozen areas. But it's a wise mom or dad who can show tolerance within reason for their "different" son or daughter. After all, if some youngsters, Thomas Edison, for example, had not been dissatisfied just to go along, we might still be using candles for light.

Some parents try to fulfill themselves in their children, egging them into situations and vocations they, themselves, desired but never had. Others don't want them to "go off on a tangent." They give them a hard time unless they hue to the "family" line, sometimes stifling the very talent with which God has endowed their son or daughter.

The flight into drugs can be a result of the intolerance of parents who insist that every child be like the one they favor most. To the one who knows he is not the favorite, this comes across as, "I don't measure up; I can't please them."

The drug crowd has low—if any—"standards for admission."

The different fellow or girl fits in with them.

Excusing Rather Than Guiding

The evasion of personal responsibility is a deadly trap which snares not only the young but too many of the alleged adults of our time. A generation has grown up in which large numbers of children have been overly protected from facing up to the harsh fact that each of us is, in large measure, the master of his fate and the captain of his soul.

Parents are providing excuses for failure instead of guidance toward overcoming failure. Cocoons are woven about their tender psyches instead of ladders for climbing out of the nest. Dependence on others is encouraged instead of teaching self-reliance, self-respect, and the simplest and most effective way of handling relationships—the Golden Rule.

Young people need to be taught to face up to problems, not look for excuses.

They Don't Need Their Children

"My parents were real cuckoos," a young woman in New York confided to a friend.

"What d'you mean?" the friend asked.

"They had us, then they just deposited us with anybody who was willing to be bothered with us," she explained. "Oh, don't get me wrong," she continued. "They were not 'child abusers' in the usual sense of the term. They just didn't need us. As far back as I can remember, I had the feeling that we interfered with our parents' pleasure in each other. As the oldest, I had to do the caring for five brothers and sisters. But nobody cared for me. Mother and Dad seemed oblivious to us, absorbed in each other. I grew up feeling worthless. If my own parents hardly seemed aware I was alive, how could I expect anybody else to love or want or accept me? That's why I turned to drugs."

An extreme instance? Maybe. But even one case is too many.

Latchkey Children

It's a grim fact that the use of drugs is becoming common in an ever lowering age group—fourth and fifth graders, or even earlier.

One explanation is that a whole host of children go home from school to an empty house. The security device commercial that begins, "Mom, I'm home," does not apply to these children.

A seven-year-old was sitting on a curb playing with a stray kitten. When a school friend asked, "Why don't you go home, Susie?" Susie said, "Nobody's home—and the kitty loves me." Susie equated Mommy's 'not being home when I come home from school' with 'Mommy doesn't love me.'

One of the most reassuring sounds is to hear an answering "Hi" when you come home and call, "Anybody home?"

Children who have no one to hurry home to, and they range in age from kindergarten through high school, are easy prey for anyone who will show them a little attention—the sex offenders, the drug pushers. We see and read accounts of missing children, some of whose mutilated bodies are later discovered, often quite near their homes; others just seem to disappear and are never heard of again. And so often the anguished parents lament, "We felt she was safe; we live just two blocks from the school—*and she had her own key.*"

Some who don't become statistics just bear the inner hurt until it gets to be too much for them.

Greg, a fourteen-year-old from an affluent suburb in the East, hung around with anybody after school. "Why should I go home?" he shrugged, "There's nobody home but the maid." He found his solace in hashish supplied by willing "friends" because he could afford their price.

Under the influence of this drug, he stole a car, a Porsche, and totalled it. He was arrested, and his mother was sent for. This became a pattern; stoned, the boy stole a car ("At least my son has class," his mother was heard to say. "He always picks expensive foreign cars."), smashed it, was arrested, and put in detention. One alert law officer suggested that Greg was a sick kid who would not be helped by prison, but who needed psychiatric help. So he was sent to a mental hospital from which he managed to escape, only to continue the destructive pattern.

By this time, his father had become terminally ill with a respiratory disease. Finally, one day the mother reached the end of her emotional rope. *"I ran away,"* she said. "I'd had it with calls from law officers, from car insurance companies, from mental hospitals. I was tired of all the responsibility, of bailing out a kid who was bent on getting into trouble, of never knowing what new problem tomorrow would bring. I ran."

She tells of a time when a doctor, concerned over her son's illness, located her and said, "What if Greg dies; what'll you do?"

"I'll bury him," she answered, mirroring her desperation.

Greg did not die. After years of intensive therapy, some of it at *Teen Challenge* where the approach is totally Christian, he is restored to a functional level of normal living. His mother, herself now a born-again, practicing Christian, is quick to admit, *"I wasn't there when Greg needed me;* now I have to live with the knowledge that the drugs he turned to have affected his mental processes irreversibly."

The hard-to-live-with-part is that *we can never turn back the clock,* no matter how much we may have learned about our behavior in the meantime.

An empty house is an invitation to all kinds of possibilities.

A mother in Huntington Beach, California, found this out just in time.

Combine a "nobody home after school" situation, a lonely twelve-year-old, time and opportunity to do what she pleases *with no supervision,* friendly classmates who likewise did not have to check in at home, and here is the scene: a noisy, giggling bunch of junior highs trooping into a townhouse complex all set for an uninhibited "good time."

In this case, the mother works in a nearby hospital, arriving home around seven in the evening. Her Carol is an only child, and the mother is raising her on her own.

The partying had gone on for some time when one neighbor said to another, "I wonder what goes on when these kids come here three or four times a week?"

"Oh, said the other, probably some junior-high club thing. They seem to be having a good time."

"Maybe, but—" and this neighbor broached the subject to Carol's mother one morning as they met at the carport. "I don't mean to be nosey, but I wonder if you know about all these young people Carol brings home so often after school. If you don't, you might want to check it out."

The mother took the hint in the right spirit and came home early

one afternoon to find eight fellows and girls lying around, som
smoking marijuana.

"Why didn't I suspect?" she said to her neighbor the next da
"How could I have been so blind?" Then she proceeded to answ
her own question. "Guess I'm so tired—working in a hospital the
days is sheer drudgery—and Carol usually has something star!
cooking for dinner; that's what I smell when I open the door. A:
way," she looked directly at the neighbor, "isn't that the last th
you would expect of your daughter, that she was in with a pe
smoking crowd? Fortunately, it made Carol sick the first time; she
just been letting the other kids come here because nobody v
home to bother them. It makes my skin crawl, though, to think wha
could have happened to her."

Not Practicing What We Preach

We've mentioned elsewhere in this book that what young people
need for effective training in values is credible models—parents
especially—who practice what they preach, whose mandate, "Do
what we say," is not invalidated by what the youngsters habitually
see.

It's one thing for a parent to warn a child of the ill effects of beer
and cigarettes; it's another for the children to believe that what
you're telling them is true, that it's not just "another no-no; something that's O.K. for adults, but not permissible for a son or daughter."

Yet, from their toddler days, most American children have stood
with a parent in a supermarket checkout line and have seen the
six-packs of beer right alongside the bottles of milk and fruit juices;
they've seen the store clerk reach for the particular brand of cigarettes the shopper asked for, and these have been stashed in with
the groceries in the brown-paper bag. In many homes, these com-
modities are stored in the refrigerator or cupboard as a matter of
course.

Said one teenager, "My dad flew into a rage and struck me when
he came home one day and saw me drinking beer from one of his
cans. But it's the first thing he reaches for when he comes home!
Mom, too, lots of times." And the kid continued in an aggrieved
tone, "If it's so good for him and Mom and their friends, why is it so
terrible for me and my friends?"

To the teenager who is desperately looking for honesty and credibility in adults, this double standard is intolerably irksome.

Assuming Without Checking

As parents, many of us tend to take it for granted that our children know and feel that they are loved and important to us. We don't just assume that their teeth are all right; we have their eyes checked; and we're careful about their general physical health. Christian parents are likewise concerned about their children's spiritual health. Why, then, do we take for granted that they feel secure in our love?

If we would make a careful, periodic check of how Johnny or Mary really feels, we might be astonished.

Some popular newspaper columns don't help in reassuring young people of their worth and importance. According to columnist Ann Landers, 70% of today's couples say that, given the same circumstances that we have in our society, they would opt not to have any children.

If they are honest with themselves, some fellows and girls know deep inside that there are still adults they can trust. But with what? With their inmost feelings? Their aspirations? Their hopes and dreams? What if their ambition for a career runs counter to what is expected of them? Can they count on a parent to understand and be supportive?

Lorene is an above average American high-school senior with good grades, a talent for playing the violin, and a love for animals. Despite the latter, her mother just wasn't prepared for Lorene's announcement, "I'm going to be a vet and work with horses."

"You must be out of your mind!" her mother exclaimed. "Think of all the advantages we've given you—and you want to waste your life working in a smelly old barn with the horses. Why can't you be normal—and *sensible?*"

The shock was understandable. Any mother might so react for the moment. But in Lorene's case, her voiced intent totally alienated her mother; she was unwilling to discuss it and trust her daughter, to hear her side. And she lost the girl.

It pays to let the child tell what he's thinking, with the freedom to explain his feelings about what he is saying.

A Maryland psychologist did, and was shocked at the response from his small daughter.

He subsequently wrote an article titled, "The Threshold of Love," and, with his kind permission, I'm sharing it with you.

There are many thresholds in life.

In the life sciences of neurology and physiology, a "threshold" is the point where a stimulus is strong enough to be perceived in the brain, and produce a response in the mechanism of the body. Individual receptors vary on the strength of a stimulus needed before the brain receives the message. People also vary in how they react to the stimulus or how they interpret a sensation once it arrives in the brain.

To illustrate this point, what happens with the threshold of pain? Not all people react alike to the same level of pain. Some may react violently to only slight pain, while others can withstand tremendous pain before they react.

What about a threshold of taste? Think of how much or how little sugar individuals use in their coffee or tea before their brain interprets the sensation transmitted from the taste receptors on the tongue for a satisfying sweetness.

In my clinical experience, I work with people who feel a lack of love in their lives. Often they are people who are genuinely loved, but for one reason or another never really felt loved; the message was "sent" but never "received." Could it be that people have their own threshold of love where a certain level of love intensity must be met before the brain perceives the message as love? I am convinced that a "Threshold of Love" does exist in the human personality.

There are at least two positively identified factors which influence and shape complex human behavior.

1. Every human being has a need to feel loved.
2. Every human being needs to have a feeling of personal worth.

If either of these factors is missing in a person's life, psychological symptoms begin to appear, and these symptoms are usually in direct proportion to perceived absence of either or both of these factors. You will notice that I used the word "perceived" in reference to the absence of love or a feeling of personal worth. There is always some difference between reality and one's perception of reality. Unfortunately, our decisions are based on the latter.

Allow me to illustrate the "Threshold of Love" with an example from my own life.

It was six years ago that I first thought of the possibility of individuals having different thresholds of response, and this was precipitated by observing the behavior of my daughter Stacie. There was never a question that my wife and I loved Stacie, and that we expressed our love to her in many ways. However, when she was about two, we started to observe Stacie manifesting specific behaviors of a psychologically abandoned child—*withdrawal, loneliness, depression, low self-concept, and signs of inner pain*. One did not have to be a trained psychologist to realize something was wrong. I also realized from a clinical point of view that most behaviors of this kind are the result of feeling unloved and/or feelings of low self-worth. Could it be our daughter either didn't feel loved or of special worth? We thought we always treated her and her brother the same, and her brother exhibited none of the negative behaviors. For the next few

66

months, my wife and I were very conscious of our ways of responding to and treating Stacie, and we could see nothing we were doing to evoke the negative behaviors we were observing. Then one evening, I remember lifting Stacie up on my lap and looking her straight in the eyes and saying, "Stacie, do you think you are an important member of our family?" With her chin still resting on her chest, her head moved from side to side indicating no. I was shocked. An empty feeling went through my entire body, and as I saw two tiny tears starting to roll down Stacie's cheeks, I could feel tears welling up in my own eyes. Then the thought struck me, *Could it be we had never reached Stacie's threshold of love response?* Since all neurological impulses operate on the "all or nothing" principle, was it possible that no love messages were getting through? If this were in fact true, it would help to explain Stacie's withdrawal behaviors. Was she actually starved for love? I can then remember hugging my daughter and telling her I did love her and that she was a very important member of our family, realizing however, that words without action are usually empty. That night I explained to my wife my conversation with Stacie, and we began to think what we could do differently. How could we get through to Stacie that we really cared and that she was special to us? Over the next few years we came up with numerous opportunities to show Stacie we loved her and that she was special to us. As a family, we began to plan one overnight family activity each month, and on a rotating basis, Stacie would get to choose where and how the family would spend our weekend away from home. Also, one day each week, Stacie would select the entire dinner menu. I can remember her requesting that I build a "clubhouse" for her and her girlfriends, like the one her brother had. So together, Stacie and I built a tree fort on top of an old picnic table, and she still uses it today. Six years have passed since that evening when I asked Stacie if she really felt loved, and I thank God for the miraculous changes we have observed in her personality. Instead of being shy and retiring, she is the "kiss bug" in the family. Now if something happens and she feels it is not fair, she speaks up instead of withdrawing. And now when I ask her if we love her and if she is an important member of our family, her answer is always enthusiastically in the affirmative. Each night when we say prayers together, Stacie hears me give thanks to God for letting her be a part of our family.

For several years now as I have presented this concept of "The Threshold of Love" to large and small audiences across the country, I have always had parents come up to me at the end of the program and say how that concept made sense to them. I have also observed that once parents consider the possibility that the love message may not be getting through to a certain family member, and start planning ways to make that person feel special, it's just a matter of time before positive things begin to happen. Sometimes the changes are in evidence within a few weeks. I have known other individuals, in which the change was not observed for several years. Yet love, like God's Word, never returns void, and therefore, the greatest commandment is that we should love one another as He has loved us (John 13:34). *(William M. Williams, Ed.D., is a certified psychologist practicing in a Christian Counseling Center in Annapolis, Maryland.)*

Being Willing to Risk Disclosure

It would pay us as well-meaning but possibly complacent parents, on the basis of this father's findings supported by his professional expertise, to do a little checking on our own children's feelings. Better to risk chagrin as one father did, than to blithely sail along on a false assumption. Paul, a man in his late thirties was raising his three sons on his own. On the surface, things were as smooth as one might expect under the circumstances: no emotional eruptions, no overt rebellion, no apparent signs the boys felt neglected or held other negative attitudes related to a one-parent home.

"Was I amazed," Paul admitted, "when one day after attending a seminar for parents without partners I decided to do some in-depth talking and listening at home! I was quite sure my sons felt loved and accepted—and I was on target with the oldest and the youngest. They were open and said things like, 'Gee, Dad, what's worryin' you? You're the greatest. We wouldn't want a better dad. Everything's OK.' But Jerry, the middle boy, was into something different. At first, he didn't contribute to our family discussion, just sat there. But, man, when he opened his mouth, it was like a sluice being opened. 'Now I'd like to have my say, Dad. Or, maybe it's best if I don't. You're not going to like it.'

" 'Try me,' I urged, and he did.

" 'We-ell—,' he hesitated then blurted out, 'I've never felt I counted for much in this family. You'd pass me over, introduce your oldest son—he mimicked me—then your baby, but me? With the others, you said their names, but for me it was, 'This is my middle kid. No name.' He went on to explain that he never got to choose, as his brothers did. It was always, 'Wait till you're older,' or 'Now you know you're too big for that. Let your little brother have it.' And so it went till Jerry ran out of steam. 'That's how it is, Dad. I sure don't feel loved and accepted, and I'm not goin' to pretend.'

"Nonplussed, caught completely by surprise, I still realized I could not let the moment pass. 'Tell me some more, Jerry,' I pleaded. 'I give you my word I was not aware of how you were feeling. If you can ever forgive me, I'll do everything in my power to make it up to you, please believe me.' "

It will take time, and this father can be sure that his son will test him to find if he really is sincere. But with this new insight as to Jerry's true feelings, together they can begin to work out a better relationship.

Once the facts are out in the open, most situations can be handled. It's imperative that parents make every effort they can to keep an open channel between themselves and their vulnerable teenagers.

Generally, teenagers will not of their own accord volunteer such disclosure of how they're feeling. They may not even be able to spell out for themselves what is eating them. They just know it's not a good feeling, they realize their parents are the cause of it, and their resentment builds up inside.

It may be hard to listen to a son's recital of the neglect and/or discrimination he's been feeling for a long time. But for the parent who dares risk it, this disclosure is the first step toward a healthy relationship between them. It can also result in a much better adjusted young man for the rest of his life. For we are later on, what we have been becoming.

Bumper Sticker Counsel

Car bumper stickers asking, "Have you hugged your kid today?" have always given me ambivolent feelings. I'm all for children being hugged—I do a lot of that—but I get irked at the thought that someone out there seems to feel I need prodding in order to do it.

Then, this very week, I wondered if I was hearing right. There was an announcement of an "electronic hugging" program; they gave the phone number, the last four "digits" K I D S, and the name of the foundation sponsoring the program.

Bless the woman and her colleagues who realize that there are countless numbers of children and young people who go day after day without even one person showing them any love or affection; without even one hug. Her innovative idea was to devise and record brief, loving messages, which through her "Dial-a-hug" ministry might meet the needs of love-starved children and young people.

It's a most commendable aim: that a child can find something, even if only on the phone, that will help to make him feel loved and wanted.

But what kind of a commentary is this on a society that has more books, more people lecturing, more seminars on how parents can and should show love to their children, than ever before in history?

We would do well to evaluate as best we can just what we are contributing to the lives of our own children. If we go overboard in any direction, let it be in expressing unconditional love, for love covers a multitude of sins.

There is no easy prescription for family life. God makes each individual with the power of choice. And as long as there is a choice to be made, some will choose one way, and some will choose another way. Two children with the same parents and the same family environment can behave drastically differently, and react in contrasting ways to the same circumstances.

We can never be certain that our children will become successful—or happy—adults. We can only try a little harder, think a little deeper, set the best example we know—and pray a little longer.

I'll NEVER
FORGIVE Myself

A decade has gone by since that October night when my youngest daughter leaped to her death. Time has helped to temper the grief, but it has not quelled the nagging WHY.

When tragedy strikes a family, almost inevitably the parents experience deep feelings of guilt. *Why? What did we do or not do?*

As I've talked with other grieving parents, I must have heard all the possible whys. Especially where drugs played a part, the questions have been these:

Why didn't I concern myself more with who my daughter's companions were?

Why did I not take more interest in how she spent her leisure time?

With all the drug talk in the news, why was I so smug as to think "It can never happen to my child"?

Why did I fail to acquaint myself with the signs of drug use?

Why was I so ill informed about the availability of drugs in the schools?

Why was I so ignorant of the effect on a young person of taking drugs?

Why—why—why—the eternal why!

Even if we had all the statistic-supported answers to all our questions, that would not bring our children back.

At the heart of our self-incriminating questions is this: *If I had been a better parent, my daughter—my son—would still be alive.*

Guilt feelings leave little room for reason or logic. You may have been an ideal parent, and yet your child fell prey to a force that robbed him of his life.

The truth is that no parent can watchdog a child 24 hours of every day. And it wouldn't be a good thing if we could or did! Nevertheless, all parents suffer guilt. No matter what happens to the child, you try to figure what you could have done to prevent it.

Many people in their grief and guilt look around for someone to blame. I know of a family that split up because of this. The father, with the best intentions in the world, suggested to his son that the boy volunteer and join the Marines rather than wait to be drafted. The son was killed in a plane crash in Hawaii (totally unrelated to any military service) and the wife, the young man's mother, bitterly blamed the father for having suggested the son join the Marine Corp.

In another instance, a 14-year-old girl was tragically drowned while at a church summer camp. The father turned on the mother with, "It's all your fault. If you were not so confoundedly holy, if you hadn't sent Peggy to that Bible camp, she would be here safe at home."

What we really are generally comes to the surface at crisis times. And blame throwing is the world's oldest form of defense mechanism. Adam blamed Eve: "It was the woman You gave me," he said to God in justification for his part in disobeying God's edict.

But there is little healing for the emotions in such blame throwing.

Nor is guilt itself productive.

It is understandable that a parent or other loved one will grieve over the loss of one who is dear to him. It's also easy to understand the fact of a certain amount of guilt.

But, to quote Dr. Maurice E. Wagner, psychologist, "The human mind is not equipped to bear a burden of guilt."

Guilt feelings paralyze us. They incapacitate us for what life demands of us daily.

When we determine, "I'll never be able to forgive myself," we're putting a life sentence on ourselves. Anyway, "never" is not a good word to heed. As Dr. Robert Schuller advises his audiences, *"Never believe NEVER."*

Harboring guilt feelings is living an "if only—" existence. We can't change the past. Hopefully we can learn from what has created the guilt feelings something that will contribute positively to the future.

Why do some people hang onto guilt?

In a sense, they may be trying to say, "See how I grieve? I can't forget, and I can't forgive myself." Is there perhaps a hint of "Other people don't feel so deeply as I do"? I wouldn't want to judge another person who has suffered, but I sometimes wonder about this. Some people go through life never smiling, as though their gloomy exterior were a monument to the deceased loved one. I know my Diane would never have wanted me to give up on the happy side of life; this would be no fitting tribute to her healthy, fun-loving way of life.

"Understanding" doesn't help.

Many well-meaning friends help to nurture the guilt feelings; they assure us, "I understand; I would feel the same if I were in your place. *I know I would never be able to forgive myself.*"

The guilty person needs something more productive than self-flagellation. Not until we can ease off that position are we on our way toward a more creative, positive handling of the problem. And we usually need other people—*the right kind of people*—to help propel us in a new direction.

Some bereaved people never get rid of guilt because there is no one around who knows how to help them. Others don't realize that it is possible for a human being to change. And in a time of severe trauma, we tend to think we will always feel as we do at that time. But we *can* come to terms with grief and guilt feelings, if we will forgive ourselves.

Why is it that of all the people we have to forgive in life, the hardest of all people to forgive is our own selves? We know because the Bible tells us that God forgives to the uttermost. Why should we not, then, believe that He wants us to accept His forgiveness and forgive ourselves? We will never know peace or be able to pursue any kind of a fulfilling life until we forgive ourselves.

Where does a father go to find solace?

Even when we appropriate God's forgiveness and thus feel for-given, the emptiness doesn't soon go away.

For me, solace came in shaking off the initial burning anger that consumed me and setting my sights on how I might help to prevent other families from having to suffer the same tragedy our family has known.

When you find out your child is on drugs, *don't waste time feeling guilty. Self-incrimination hobbles both you and your children.*

Guilt paralyzes what the Chinese sages called "right action." Although it may be cathartic, self-castigation appears to the young as self-pity and impotence. It is contagious. It contaminates the entire household. There is a difference between legitimate guilt and legitimate grief or concern; guilt is often a disguised form of blame; it forces the young to retreat, to draw away—for they and you both know that they caused your pain.

When a drug crisis or problem becomes public knowledge, guilt often shades into shame. Parents worry about what people will think, about the "repercussions." Excessive concern about public opinion or neighborhood gossip is a kind of betrayal of the young. It infects the household with unnecessary tension, self-doubt, and anxiety; and it denies to the young what they need most: a sense of ungrudging support, stability, and strength—and the feeling that personal needs and affection are more important than what people think.

My wife and I decided that our family was strong enough and Christian enough to bear up under the pressure of relating the truth behind Diane's death.

It's a rare headliner that lasts more than a day or so. So you can console yourself that, although your son or daughter's name, your "shame" is on people's lips today, they'll have someone else's troubles to engage their minds tomorrow.

Let's squelch guilt. Let's concentrate on helping the child. I could not have done it alone; at least, it would have taken much longer for me to work through the guilt and anger. As I've described in another part of this book, God used Dr. Norman Vincent Peale to channel His message to me, to give new purpose to my life. It was then I learned that if I would stop my futile dwelling on something I could not change, and lift my head and look toward tomorrow in a positive way, my daughter would not have died in vain.

My ability as a communicator had brought laughter to many lives and homes. I had an audience who would listen to me. Now I could put my God-given talent as an entertainer to another use.

This was where I could pick up my life and start over, as Dr. Peale had urged. Apart from this new, sane view of my daughter's death, I might still be wallowing in a sea of crippling rage and guilt.

It's my prayer that other similarly bereaved, hurting parents will be helped, *that they will let God help them,* to open their hearts and their eyes and realize that they have a job to do. It's ironic but true that grief can singularly qualify and equip us to be specialists in helping others.

Hanging onto guilt, saying, "I can never forgive myself," will nullify our ability to help others. Someone else can be inspired to rise up from the depths of grief because you and I have dared with God's help to attempt to take such steps.

High purpose is not enough.

Realization that there was something I could do did not make this a reality. By no means. I was possessed of a high and noble purpose, no question about that. The crusading spirit was strong in me. But, worthy as that is, it can quickly dissipate without action. What I needed was a program, a way to go. But first, I desperately needed information. I knew how to talk to people; now I needed to learn what to tell them.

I'm still learning. And the sharing of what I've found out about drugs, the victims of drugs, and those who get rich by trafficking in drugs has absorbed my time and interest these past ten years.

I've been too occupied to dwell on guilt.

I still don't have the milk of human kindness for drug traffickers; my forgiveness does not extend to them. (I favor life imprisonment for the convicted drug trader and supplier.) Nevertheless, with the help of God, I've been able to take the tragedy of my daughter's death, shape it like a missile, and use it. If, through my efforts I can save only one life, I'll think to myself, *That could have been my daughter!*

We can't afford to be lukewarm in our battle against this evil. For drug abuse has gone beyond epidemic proportions in this country.

The hardest thing for me to answer is the question, "What can I do?" And many come to me with this question. You may be asking the same question. Well, there's no precise spot to which I can allocate you. It isn't like an army in which you can join a squad and fight. *You've got to do whatever you can in your own community, your own neighborhood, your own home.*

If you are one of the parents who's beating yourself over the head, saying over and over, "Where did I fail my child? Why did he turn to drugs? How can I ever forgive myself?" I have this to say to you. You are compounding a problem; whether or not the guilt is yours, there is absolutely nothing to be gained by sitting around moaning and groaning, "If only—!"

I've heard, I suppose, in these ten years, all the "if onlys," and I've had my own litany along those lines, believe me. But let me say to you, kindly, "if only" is a dead-end street; it leads to nowhere. And meantime, every morning you and I wake up, more and more of our young people have had their first experiences with dope.

All of us need to shove the guilty thoughts far from us and utilize our mental and emotional energy, marshal our thinking into ways we can contribute to the solution.

The Best Way to BEAT DRUGS

Before we submit a remedy, we have to pinpoint the disease. We not only have a drug problem; *we have a people problem.*

Today, because of careless prescriptions for every kind of mind-bending psychoactive drug, and the forces of advertising and selling, most of us believe that relief from any kind of worry is just a swallow away.

Our medicine cabinets are stuffed with uppers and downers and tranquilizers. Many of our youngsters think nothing of dropping out with LSD or mescaline, of sniffing glue, of smoking pot.

And of course we all know that the two great drugs which kill more people than all others combined, by far, are nicotine and alcohol. They continue to grow, socially acceptable, advertisable (albeit with restrictive warning labels!), used worldwide.

I repeat, we have a people problem. There will always be drugs; there always have been. Even the cavemen had their roots, their mushrooms and berries, powerful enough to fortify them against what awaited them when they stepped out of their caves.

Why do people, young and old, use drugs?

Elsewhere in this book we've discussed a number of reasons why kids and others "turn on." One strong motivating factor we may not have submitted is the sheer pleasure many get out of taking drugs. They take them, in whatever form, for the pleasure it gives them. Oh, it may be to relieve pain or boredom, anger or frustration—or lone-liness. But, boiled down, they use the drug to get a better feeling than they presently have.

When are they going to stop using drugs? Not until people find something else that makes them feel better than taking drugs does; not a "constructive alternative"; not one more "no-no." You can go around for the rest of your life telling children and older people that taking drugs is bad for them. But when you tell them what they can do to make themselves feel better, you are beginning to hit a more constructive alternative.

The Great Alternative

The best constructive alternative to taking drugs is Christianity, belief in God.

I've seen all the other things. I've seen methadone, which is nothing but taking a person off one drug and putting him on another cheaper, more available, more easily supervised drug.

I have seen people taken off all kinds of drugs, legal and illegal, with the use of psychiatry. Long sessions with psychologists and psychiatrists relieve their inner guilts temporarily, and get them off drugs. Then another crisis comes along—a divorce, a death, the loss of a job, a long sickness, anxiety, depression (which is becoming more prevalent every day, in all ages)—and they are back to the drugs!

Psychiatry, as far as a remedy for drug dependency is concerned, is a kind of Band-Aid that covers over the problem. Then, when the next bout of serious depression or loneliness strikes, the person unerringly remembers what drugs can do to iron out the wrinkles of life and push off the worries—and he goes back to them.

You can put the person in a half-way house, and as long as he is supported by the structure of other drug users—former drug users principally, and wonderful, well-meaning people—he is all right. But when you take him away from that supportive atmosphere and put him out into the community where once again he meets the same people and circumstances which contributed to his "downfall," he tends to drop back into the same problems he had before. (A classic case in the news last year was a well-known entertainer's daughter, who after having had a number of months free from drugs as the result of spending time in a rehabilitation center, slipped back into the habit. She was sent back to the same place in the hope that she would be completely set free from the bondage of drugs and be able to take up her life again. My heart goes out to this girl, and her parents who are doing the thing they think is best for her, wholly with the daughter's welfare at heart.

But, if this is their only hope, it's a broken reed they are putting their trust in.

The One Way

There is only one way that I know of to gain permanent release from the power of drugs. For old and young alike, the only way for 24-hours a day, year-in and year-out release is Jesus Christ. It's that simple. And yet, it's that difficult, because some people find it impossible to admit that this is the way, to confess it, to accept it.

I have made movies with Nicky Cruz, former leader of the Mau Mau Gang in New York, who became a follower of Christ, and is now a preacher. I've been with Nicky down in the ghettos of New York where we talked with heroin-ridden former gang members whose lives were blown. I have travelled with the Teen Challenge group, and Youth for Christ and Campus Crusade for Christ groups.

I have been in meetings with Street Christians, and with so-called "Jesus Freaks"—kids who are getting off drugs, and getting "high" on Christianity—to the same degree that they did before on drugs.

I've seen this whole group of struggling, believing, hopeful young people whose lives are changed—changed not just for the immediate like a temporary "miracle"—but changed permanently. How? Because when these Christian organizations reach young people and adults, they put into their lives a meaningful belief and acceptance of Christ. Then, the worries and problems and frustrations of life, the bewilderments and defeats, become shared with a friend. That's what most of us need, a good friend who is always with us.

That is why, after all these years of meeting with the top drug experts of the world on the subject of drug abuse, I have come to this solid conclusion. We need to approach life as a great challenge, and a great problem with which we need help. And help comes from above.

There will always be drugs. The laboratories are now busy changing the alkaloids and the compounds to make more and more mind-bending drugs which will be available to us. We will never stop that.

What we must do is to come back to the teachings of the Bible, come back to the teachings of the love of Christ and love one for another. When we do this, we are at the root of the problem, the problem being human beings who cause these problems.

Christianity fills a person's life with hope and faith—two things that most of the young people on drugs feel they never had. So, once a kid is hooked on drugs, the very best thing to get him off is Christianity.

It's very encouraging to see the phenomenal growth of interest in religion among young people. And a good deal of this is in a sense a by-product of the drug culture which itself is frequently a backlash at the money-grabbing clawing for possessions. In our hearts we know that what Jesus said is true, that "a man's life consists not in the things he possesses" (Luke 12:15). There are better "things" than these, and young people are in the forefront of those who are finding them.

I've been in a number of churches in southern California where, on any Sunday, you will see hundreds—maybe even a thousand or more—of the most joyful girls and fellows and young adults you will ever see anywhere. They have a peace, a serenity about them. They're outgoing and friendly. From varied economic and social backgrounds, many of them have one thing in common: they have come out of the drug culture. Someone has introduced them to the One who never turned any needy person away. They have found in Him, and in the fellowship of His people, something better than drugs. Sold on Christianity, feeding on the Bible, they are out to win others from the snare of drugs, offering them with the credibility of their own experience the only lasting "cure." Having had good nurturing themselves, they pass this on to the new convert. It's a little bit of Heaven to be in their midst and hear them sing such Christian songs as "He is Lord." (For once drugs was lord of their lives.)

It would be an eye-opener to some of the pessimists who shake their heads over "the young people of today," if they would step into such a church. When I could be depressed over the fact that numerically, we're losing by the day, by the hour, as the drug interests forge their chains to bind our kids, I take heart knowing that *some are being saved.*

We all need to be credible; we need to package our faith so that people are attracted to Christianity. We need—I say it reverently—to be "pushers." We have the product; we can afford to share it.

Why are so many who believe that Jesus saves from everything, even drug addiction, so silent, or so negative that they do not attract the very people who need what they have?

In the matter of our attitude toward those who have become addicted (I really don't like the word "addict;" they are *persons* who have become victims of drug abuse) we can learn a lot from this prayer in the *Book of Common Prayer.*

For the Victims of Addiction

O blessed Lord, You ministered to all who came to You; Look with compassion upon all who through addiction have lost their health and freedom. Restore to them the assurance of your unfailing mercy; remove from them the fears that beset them; strengthen them in the work of their recovery; and to those who care for them, give patient understanding and persevering love. Amen.

The *Book of Common Prayer* (1977 edition, p. 831—Oxford University Press, New York.)

Is EDUCATION
the Answer?

Forewarned is always forearmed. "Know your enemy" is a priority strategy. So, yes, education concerning drugs is an answer. But we need to define "education" and think about who will teach whom, and how?

Horrified at finding her younger daughter, junior-high Kathy, had been smoking marijuana, a mother turned to her married daughter, herself not long out of school. "I just can't believe it, Barbara," she said, "but her teacher told me it's been going on for weeks."

"But, Mom, you must have smelled it," Barbara answered.

The mother looked appalled. Defensively, she countered, "How would you expect me to be able to identify drugs by their smell—or any other sign? And how would that help, if I did? What Kathy needs is to repent and give it up."

Now I'm not here to judge that mother. She was likely traumatized at the thought that her child had been caught in the drug trap. But I would say this to her and to other parents who are bent out of shape at their kids getting into drugs:

Don't insist that your children repent when what they need is your help.

In their zeal to keep the young away from drugs, just when they need our help, adults often try to increase their sense of shame. They pressure and frighten them, hoping that their consciences and anxieties will keep them in line. If we catch them using drugs, make them pay; we exact a forfeit, a penance. We ask them to earn our attention and demonstrate their good intentions by admitting their past mistakes.

This is understandable. We may have been brought up this way, but if we'll cast our minds back, we'll admit that this was not the response that motivated us to want to do better either.

The young need help and support from parents and other adults—not "justice"; not even forgiveness (at that time). Adults demean the young when they insist on a confession. If they submit (without feeling truly repentant) they diminish themselves; they feel dishonest. If they refuse to confess, they are forced into postures of rebellion. It is often hard for the young to ask for help—even when they want and need it—for it seems to them a kind of weakness. In such situations, *they need respect for who they are regardless of what they have done;* they need support; they need demonstrated affection.

The great bulk of average American parents, unless they live in a drug-enlightened community (usually one where the blight has struck and they're trying to fight it), are naive about drugs. This despite available information. On the subject of marijuana, for instance, there's a group in Stamford, Connecticut, *Citizens for Informed Choices on Marijuana.* Among the literature they distribute is a packet, *Helping Your Child Resist the Marijuana Culture.* This includes *Marijuana in Our Schools, What Every Parent Can Do About Marijuana, Parents Talk to Their Children About Marijuana, and If You Don't, Who Will?* (The address of this group is CICOM, 300 Broad Street, Stamford, Connecticut 06901.) Writers of the material are physicians, health-care professionals, and parents. They suggest that "The parents finding their child—and increasingly the age is dropping—is involved with marijuana or any other drug, should immediately seek information. They should also commit themselves intellectually and emotionally to a firm stand and a long haul. It may take several months to get the child drug free."

Many communities undoubtedly have the resources to start a fight-back program. It usually takes a sufficiently aroused parent to get it going. This is infinitely more productive than turning our energy toward ways to punish our own children.

Drugs are not a fad. They are not going to go away. So parents, teachers, and other concerned adults need to arm themselves with valid information.

Signs and Signals

One of the first items of information a parent needs is an understanding of what to look for in a marijuana user; how to recognize it. The effects of marijuana vary widely, but it is generally conceded that these are the recognizable signs:

• *Lack of appetite.* Especially in a teenage boy, this trait should alert the aware mother. It may differ with girls due to their engrossment with keeping their weight down. Even so, when normal, healthy youngsters show a marked disinterest in food, mealtime after mealtime, it calls for concern.

• *Short attention span.* By the time your children are in their teens, you know their habits and usual procedures. When your son or daughter who normally can be counted on to finish his/her homework, to remain absorbed in a hobby for a reasonable time, to play and concentrate on a game and finish it, suddenly changes in this respect, it's time to give thought to *why the change.* Why the break-away attention, why the restlessness and hopping from one thing to another? This could well signal that your son or daughter is involved with drugs.

• *Slothfulness or lethargy.* Again, it's the unusual degree of a given new behavior we're thinking about. All young people are "lazy" at times (in fact all of us need times to do nothing, without being challenged or rebuked). But when a normally eager, active, enthusiastic boy or girl suddenly and consistently "can't be bothered," the parents should question the cause(s).

• *Drowsiness* is another suspicious sign of drug usage.

• *Drunken appearance.* A person on drugs may clown, take over the conversation, and be uncontrollably hilarious when the occasion doesn't warrant it. He may express foolish opinions; he may use profanity, which he would never do "in his right mind"; he may be glaringly untruthful in the hope of covering up and avoiding suspicion. In all, the only thing missing is the smell of liquor on his breath!

• *Loss of memory.* The inability to remember important details often marks the experienced pot smoker. Tied into this is dullness and disorder of thought, and a groping for the right words: poor verbalization.

• *Impaired judgment,* is both a sign and an effect of using marijuana. The ramifications can be horrendous, as when a young driver who is on drugs and whose judgment is lessened is at the wheel of a car. The impaired judgment leads to a loss of inhibitions, a forgetting that he may not be the world's best driver. He thinks he is, and acts accordingly, sometimes with deadly consequences.

• *Staying away from home* for unexplained lengths of time is something the parent should always question, but more so if it is accompanied by some of the other signs we've mentioned. Also, when your boy or girl starts to try *selling some possessions,* be on the alert.

A good rule to follow is this: be suspicious of any sudden change that is completely out of character for the individual.

Be vigilant. Don't delude yourself that drugs happen only to other people's kids. Know your child well enough that you can differentiate between usual and unusual behavior, attitude, moods. This may call for spending more time with him. I think it was Dr. James Dobson, physician, psychologist, and father, who said, "The average American father spends 37 seconds a day with his son."

Let the young people help.

In the realm of drug information, as in every other area, children and young people certainly need to be educated. But who will they listen to? And to what? They're not listening to the adults who quote reams of statistics to them in an attempt to frighten them away from drugs. They won't listen to moralizing.

Sometimes they learn most and fastest from their peers.

"What? Encourage them to listen to their peers," I hear some people argue. "Why, it's from their schoolmates and 'friends' they learn all the bad they know."

This may or may not be true. However, some communities have had success through student-led workshops. As early as 1969, a Dallas high school, Brian Adams High, held a two-day workshop, and reported: Students at Brian Adams High are learning, under student leadership, the ramifications of the "turned on" generation. They're learning how to identify drugs, to recognize the signs and the smells, to know what a "bad trip" is like, and what the law says about taking drugs.

Said Robert T. Davis, executive director of the Texas Law Enforcement and Youth Development Foundation, "If you want the young people to support an antidrug program, they've got to help create it."

"If there is just one drug user in the school, there is a need for a drug program," said Davis, who has taken the workshop to more than 25,000 students. "It's a preventive program," he explains and adds, "The students are really enthusiastic."

What if the school will not cooperate?

Schools exist for the good of the community, and for the most part they act in the interests of pupils and parents.

A suburban Philadelphia woman stormed into the principal's office.

"You knew my son was on drugs," she accused the principal, "yet you didn't tell his father and me." Before the man could answer or explain the circumstances, she ranted on, "If the boy had needed glasses, you would have notified us. But when he's smoking marijuana, you leave us to find out for ourselves. Was it not your duty to inform us?"

When she momentarily halted her tirade, the principal cut in. "May I tell you what 'doing our duty' brought us? Law suits. Most parents do not want to hear, 'Your son/your daughter is using drugs'; they don't believe us. They would rather hide their heads in the sand."

It's a bitter comment on today's society that so much good goes undone because people who would be helpful are afraid of what will happen if they try. We need some Good Samaritans who will brave the odds, like the one who stopped to help an ostracized victim just because he was a victim.

Two Schools of Thought

"Should the schools teach our children about drugs?" one mother asked another.

"Definitely not," the other replied. "That's where my Allan learned about drugs! While the film was designed to warn young people, my son was taking lessons from it. He learned the drug lingo. He found out how the kids got the dope; how they evaded letting their parents know they were on it—a lot of information I wish he had never been exposed to."

"Then you're against teaching about drugs in school?" the first mother probed. "What about for parents? Don't you think we need to be taught how to recognize the signs, and how to react if—God forbid—one of our children should ever get trapped?"

"Agreed," said the second mother. "We need to find out all we possibly can from the school, and from other agencies as well."

This mother learned too late what "drug education" could do for the kid in the classroom, but she didn't keep quiet. She urged school authorities to look at their responsibility in regard to teaching films and other drug education.

How soon is soon enough?

I encourage teachers to start at the second or third grade level with a no-nonsense, no-mythology, no-panic, no-moralizing inclusion of drug education. I advocate it as part of hygiene and physical education. "You teach the children not to run out on the street with their eyes shut," I tell them, "and you teach them not to set fire to their clothing, and not to put anything in their mouths without knowing what it is. Why, then, should you not teach them about drugs?"

Drug education, loosely speaking, was my primary object in going out and making public speeches. As fast as I could learn from the experts—I began to be an expert on experts—I tried to pass along this teaching. Not only in schools, but wherever the opportunity presented itself: in town halls, churches, civic auditoriums, in Washington to a number of men in high places, and to the United Nations. My main thrust was toward reaching our young people.

By the high-school years, even junior-high in many parts of the country, it's too late. Attitudes have been formed. Sometimes misinformation has muddied the waters, and the older kids are not ready to listen. We need to start earlier than that. If we can endue young children with a sense of pride in having a healthy body, then maybe we'll be able to instill some productive attitudes toward the evil of drugs.

School is the place to learn many things. But when it comes to something that can influence a student for the rest of his life, that's the parents' business. They have a right to view films prior to their being shown to their sons and daughters.

Here is where the PTA and other parent organizations need to wield their influence. They should crusade for the right of parents to preview films that are to be used to educate their children. (This is as true of sex education as of drug films.)

Drug use and loose sex go hand in hand in many of today's schools. I've lived long enough not to be too easily shocked, but I could hardly believe my ears when I heard this announcement:

"Among our school supplies, you will find early pregnancy detection kits," and this was an ad for *elementary* school supplies!

What does it take to arouse us?

For me, it was the death of my loved youngest daughter.

For a family in Florida, it was learning that not only was their daughter smoking pot, she was also dating a dealer who was using her to gain entrance to her high-school crowd.

For another mother, indignation boiled over when, on a shopping trip, she ran into a "supermarket of drug paraphernalia" in her neighborhood. Among the products, she found an assortment of unbelievable "toys": footballs and plastic space guns transformed into "power hitters" that blast marijuana smoke into the lungs; pens that double as pot devices; candy Quaaludes; kiddie belt buckles and skateboards for hiding your "stash," and comic books showing how to cut and snort cocaine.

These and other parents, shocked into the realization that there is a very real drug menace, and that their children can be easily drawn into it, are banding together in many communities. They're learning what they need to know about drugs, and they're doing something about the problem.

It's time they did, for marijuana smoking among high-school seniors climbed 80% between 1975 and 1978. Even more frightening in its portent is the fact that as early as fourth and fifth grade, some children are now on pot.

What defense do parents have against the menace? What realistic steps can they take to halt the upsurge?

• *Know your children's friends.*

As much as possible, keep an open house for your children's friends. Treat them warmly, show an interest in them. Feed them. The rapport you establish with the friends will strengthen the ties with your own boy and girl.

You may not like each one; some may not be the kind of friends you would select for your children. But, by knowing who and what kind of person each one is, you have "armor" you would never have were you to shun them. And, who knows, you may be able to exert a good influence on these friends, a double bonus for your efforts.

When parents of children in trouble call me, I advise, "Check out their friends." My Diane was an adventurous child. She was the youngest of five, and since ours was a loving family, and the other four were okay, we took too much for granted. She wanted to be an actress (she had everything going for her: looks, talent, personality) and she ran around with show business kids. They're a pretty undisciplined group who seek out drama schools and acting because it's fun. It's taking the easy way out. I should say that they're not all like that, but the ones Diane ran with were.

Friends are the most powerful influence in your child's life. Don't ever underestimate that. When I started on my crusade, I was out to get the pushers. To my dismay, I learned that many of them were the kids themselves; and some of them were missionary in their zeal to introduce their friends to drugs. I repeat, know who your son and daughter's friends are.

- *Establish a loving dictatorship in your home.*

Set limits. Life is full of restrictions of one kind or another, and the child who has lived with known, spelled-out limits, is better prepared to face the frustrations of life.

Sometimes I wonder if parents had all parked their minds somewhere when they went hook, line, and sinker for the permissiveness line, swallowing it whole. This country is still reaping the whirlwind of what was sowed through permissive parents. God gave children parents to train them, and training calls for some No's; some "You can'ts" as well as loving guidance. I've heard it said—and I believe it—that the child who has never been taught to obey his parents will have a hard time obeying God.

It's the loving parent who says as Tom or Sally goes off for the evening, "We'll be counting on you to be home by the right time"—the right time having been set, an appropriate hour for the occasion, and the youngster knowing that you really mean it.

You can expect static from the normal teenager; he'll come up with, "But Mom, Dad, none of the other kids have to be home at (whatever the hour)." "You're not 'other kids' " is all you need reply; no argument. I've met many parents who've admitted, "I wish I'd had the guts to set some rules and stick with them, but it was always such a hassle." Nobody said that raising kids is without its hassles.

Also, there's growing evidence that young people admire authority and loathe permissiveness, that they long for the establishment and enforcement of moral standards.

It's important that there be a clear channel so that if something prevents even the most conscientious teenager from arriving home on time, he be allowed to explain the circumstances. *Kids need to be trusted.* They need to know we expect the best from them, not that we're always waiting to pounce on them for an infraction of our rules. Many a kid has been turned in the wrong direction by such behavior on the part of his parents. Nevertheless, *parents should be in charge.* As I've heard Clyde Narramore say, "The father is the chairman of the board in his own home."

Be a dictator if you like, but let it be a loving dictatorship. Don't just "lay down the law." Talk over things. Kids want to know what and where the guidelines are, that their parents really care enough to set limits.

- *Learn something of the lingo.*

"I don't know what young people are talking about anymore," a mother complained to me. "Seems they have a language of their own."

She's right. It's hard to keep up with their lingo. But it will pay parents to acquaint themselves with at least some of the terms as they apply to the drug scene.

Here are some of the names by which young people and adults refer to various kinds of dope. (These may change and others be added by the time you are reading this, but it will help you to recognize that the topic is drugs): *Bennies, Chalk whites, Uppers, Dexies, Speed, Meth, Crystals, Reds, Yellows, Rainbows, Blues, Pot, Grass, Weed, Joints, Hash, Acid, STP, PCP, LSD, Stuff, Smack, Coke.*

These are code names for drugs, some of which are prescribed by the family physician to be used only for the patient. In the hands of any other person, they are illegal drugs.

It's not enough to say to your teenager that using drugs is a bad thing. You need scientific proof. How do you obtain this? From the Department of Health, Education and Welfare in Washington, D.C., or from any city or state health department. There's no scarcity of material. Along with getting this into the young people's hands, here's something else you can do. Around the dinner table, bring up newspaper items that verify what the literature says. One reason my wife and I gave Diane's story to the newspapers is that we want parents, we want kids to read about it and be shocked, be frightened at what can happen to a drug user.

Since Diane's death, I've been invited to testify before the National Crime Commission and a U.S. Senate committee, as well as to the U.N. I've studied and learned all I can, so that in turn I can help to educate other people.

Education is not the great final answer to the problem of drug addiction. But, without knowledge, our efforts to curb it can only fail. We'll just be beating the air; we'll be running around making noises no one is paying any heed to.

Anything a parent or other concerned adult can do—anything at all—to save even one child from becoming a victim of drugs, is the very least we can do.

So let's arm ourselves with knowledge, then attack on all fronts.

PART TWO: Statistics

Drug Use on
THE COLLEGE CAMPUS

Drug use continues to be a serious problem on the college campuses of America, with marijuana use at a high point and little change noted in the use of amphetamines, barbiturates, and hallucinogens.

Since the late '60s the percentage of students saying they have tried marijuana has grown from 5 percent in 1967 and 55 percent in 1974 to 66 percent in 1980. And the proportions saying they have tried amphetamines, barbiturates, and hallucinogens are virtually the same today as in the early seventies.

In a 1970 survey, 16 percent of a nationwide sample of college students said they had tried amphetamines (speed, etc.). Just one year later the comparable figure was 22 percent. In the current survey, 21 percent say they have tried these drugs.

In 1969, one-tenth of the college population (10 percent) said they had tried barbiturates (Quaaludes, etc.). By 1970, the figure had increased to 15 percent, where it remained in 1971. In the current survey, the proportion is one in seven—14 percent.

In terms of hallucinogens (LSD, mescaline, etc.), 1 percent of the student population said they tried these drugs in 1967. Two years later, the figure was up to 4 percent. Then came a sharp jump in the number who had tried these drugs—to 14 percent in 1970 and 18 percent in 1971. Today's figure is 14 percent.

The current survey also sought to determine how many college youths have experimented with cocaine (or "coke") and "angel dust" (PCP). The figures are 15 percent and 8 percent, respectively.

More Frequent Users

The current Gallup audit of drug usage also focused on more frequent users of amphetamines, barbiturates, and hallucinogens—that is, those saying they have used these drugs in the last 30 days. While the current figures are lower than those recorded at the beginning of the decade, it should again be stressed that drug use persists as a serious problem in America's colleges and universities.

In 1970, 6 percent of college students said they had used amphetamines in the last 30 days. The next year, the figure was 8 percent. Today it is 5 percent.

The trend in use of barbiturates shows 5 percent having used the drugs in the last 30 days in 1970, 4 percent in 1971, and 3 percent in the latest survey.

The number saying they had used hallucinogens in the last 30 days was 6 percent in 1970, 4 percent in 1971, and 2 percent today.

The current survey also sought to determine how many college students have used cocaine or PCP in the last 30 days. The figures are 5 percent and 1 percent, respectively.

These questions were asked:
"Which of the items listed on this card, if any, have you, yourself EVER used?
Used within the last 12 months?
Used within the last 30 days?"
The card listed the following:
Amphetamines (Speed, etc.)
Barbiturates (Quaaludes, etc.)
Hallucinogens (LSD, mescaline, etc.)
Cocaine
"Angel dust" (PCP)
Following are the results:

Ever Tried Amphetamines?

1970	16%
1971	22%
LATEST	21%

Ever Tried Barbiturates?

1969	10%
1970	15%
1971	15%
LATEST	14%

Ever Tried Hallucinogens?

1967	1%
1969	4%
1970	14%
1971	18%
LATEST	14%

Ever Tried Cocaine?

LATEST	15%

Ever Tried Angel Dust?

LATEST	8%

Used Amphetamines in Last 30 Days?

1970	6%
1971	8%
LATEST	5%

Used Barbiturates in Last 30 Days?

1970	5%
1971	4%
LATEST	3%

Used Hallucinogens in Last 30 Days?

1970	6%
1971	4%
LATEST	2%

Use by Class in College

The proportion of college students who say they have tried the drugs listed in the survey increases steadily from freshman to senior years. For example, 74 percent of freshmen say they have never used any of the drugs compared to 59 percent among seniors.

The differences by class, however, are not so marked in terms of frequency of use, indicating that drug use on our campuses may be tapering off.

The following tables show the differences by class in college:

Percent Saying Ever Used
(By class in college)

	Fresh.	Soph.	Jr.	Sr.	All Classes
Amphetamines	17%	21%	28%	31%	21%
Barbiturates	12%	16%	15%	16%	14%
Hallucinogens	10%	15%	16%	21%	14%
Cocaine (coke)	13%	14%	18%	23%	15%
Angel Dust	6%	9%	10%	9%	8%
None	74%	72%	66%	59%	70%
No answer	3%	2%	3%	4%	3%

Percent Saying Used in Last 30 Days
(By class in college)

	Fresh.	Soph.	Jr.	Sr.	All Classes
Amphetamines	5%	6%	7%	4%	5%
Barbiturates	2%	3%	2%	3%	3%
Hallucinogens	2%	2%	3%	3%	2%
Cocaine (coke)	4%	4%	7%	8%	5%
Angel Dust	*	1%	*	1%	*
None	8%	8%	6%	9%	8%
No answer	2%	3%	4%	7%	3%

*Less than one percent

MARIJUANA:
Who Smokes It?

The percentage of Americans who have tried marijuana has doubled during the last four years, with one adult in four having now tried "grass" at least once.

In the latest Gallup survey of marijuana use in America, 24 percent of the nation's adults, 18 and older, report they've sampled the substance at least once. Half, 12 percent, can be considered recent users, having last tried it during the past year.

The overall usage figure is double what it was in 1973, and six times what it was in 1969, when the Gallup Poll's first survey of marijuana found only 4 percent had tried it.

Most Likely Users

As has consistently been the case, young adults in the latest survey are more likely to be users than those in any other population group. Fully 56 percent of those under 30 years of age (and 59 percent of those between 18 and 24) say they have tried marijuana. Among people between 30 and 49 years old, the percentage who have tried it (16 percent) is less than one-third that of young people. And with those over 50 years old, only 5 percent have indulged.

Sex and educational background present interesting contrasts.

Men (31 percent) continue to be more likely to have tried marijuana than women (17 percent). And those with college training include more who have used it (36 percent) than people whose education stopped at the high-school level (23 percent) or grade-school level (5 percent).

One of the largest and most interesting differences is that between whites and nonwhites. In 1973, the percentage of whites and nonwhites who had tried marijuana was about the same. Today, the level among nonwhites (36 percent) is significantly higher than that of whites (22 percent).

To determine what percentage of Americans have used marijuana at least once, the following question was asked:

"Have you, yourself, ever happened to try marijuana?"

The following table shows how the use of marijuana has climbed since 1969:

Ever Tried Marijuana?

TODAY	24%
1973	12%
1972	11%
1969	4%

And here are the latest national findings as well as those by major population groups:

	Today	1973	Change since 1973
NATIONAL	24%	12%	+12%
Men	31%	16%	+15%
Women	17%	8%	+ 9%
Whites	22%	12%	+10%
Nonwhites	36%	13%	+23%
College	36%	22%	+14%
High school	23%	12%	+11%
Grade school	5%	2%	+ 3%
Under 30 years old	56%	36%	+20%
18-24 years	59%	41%	+18%
25-29 years	51%	26%	+25%
30-49 years old	16%	5%	+11%
50 years and older	5%	2%	+ 3%

Current Users

A second question in the current survey sought to determine what percentage of Americans are presently using marijuana.

Analysis of the results indicates half of those who say they have tried marijuana at least once have done so during the last year. Among the various population groups, those with the highest over-all percentage of users are also most likely to have the highest percentage of current users—young people, the college-educated, men, and nonwhites.

Here is the question asked followed by the results:

About how long ago did you last try marijuana?

	During the last week	During the last month	During the last year	Ever used
NATIONAL	6%	8%	12%	24%
Men	7%	9%	14%	31%
Women	4%	5%	9%	17%
Whites	4%	5%	10%	22%
Nonwhites	13%	16%	20%	36%
College	10%	12%	20%	36%
High school	4%	6%	10%	23%
Grade school	1%	1%	1%	5%
Under 30 years	15%	20%	30%	56%
18-24 years	17%	22%	36%	59%
25-29 years	11%	15%	20%	51%
30-49 years	2%	3%	7%	16%
50 & older	*	*	1%	5%

*Less than 1 percent

Teens: Marijuana's Easy to Get

In a recent Gallup Youth Survey, three out of four American young people between the ages of 13 and 18 said that it was either very easy (35 percent) or fairly easy (40 percent) for students at their school to obtain marijuana. Fewer than one in five teens (19 percent) said it was difficult to do so, while the balance of 6 percent didn't know.

The following tongue-in-cheek remarks from a 16-year-old boy, while admittedly facetious, corroborate that it is indeed easy to obtain marijuana at many schools:

"My school has an enrollment of about 2,500, and it seems to me everyone in school either smokes pot or pushes it. Smoking seems to be practically the only form of entertainment in our town."

In a more serious vein, a 15-year-old girl said:

"A lot of people get it from older brothers or sisters, and then share it with friends. There is always someone who can get you marijuana."

Not surprisingly, the age group to which an individual teenager belongs is a crucial factor in the ease or difficulty with which he or she thinks marijuana can be obtained.

For example, 81 percent of high-school students said it was at least fairly easy for students to keep supplied, while only 59 percent of junior-high schoolers thought this was so.

Of equal importance in determining the ease of obtaining marijuana is the area of the country in which the teenager lives. Teens living in the East and far West are quite a bit more likely to say their fellow students can get marijuana easily than are youngsters from the Midwest and South.

The size of the community in which a teenager lives also has a bearing on availability. Teens who live in the central cities and their suburbs are apt to have an easier time obtaining marijuana than are their counterparts from rural areas. It is perhaps belaboring the obvious to note that teenagers who have tried marijuana are considerably more likely to say it's easy for kids at their schools to get it than youngsters who haven't used the substance. However, even among nonusers, two out of three (67 percent), say it's at least fairly easy to obtain it at their schools.

Two other questions in the survey series sought teenage opinion on comparisons between the use of alcohol and marijuana—both as sources of enjoyment and as health hazards.

In each instance, alcohol comes off second best, being thought by teenagers to be less enjoyable than marijuana by a wide margin, and also, by better than a two-to-one ratio, being thought of as the more dangerous of the two to young people's health.

For the teenage sample as a whole, 43 percent feel that marijuana is more enjoyable for young people, while 28 percent believe this to be true of alcohol. Of the remainder, 10 percent think there is no difference between the two, and 19 percent do not express an opinion.

With regard to the relative health hazards of the two, alcohol was thought the more dangerous by 58 percent of teens, while less than one-half that proportion, 25 percent, believe marijuana deserved the "more dangerous" designation. Fourteen percent of teenagers see no difference between the two substances as far as health is concerned.

It is interesting to note that even among teenagers who have never tried marijuana, it gets the nod over alcohol as being more enjoyable, by a narrow 36 to 31 percent difference, although as many as one-fourth of nonusers (24 percent) do not venture an opinion in this regard. Similarly, nonusers are more inclined to find alcohol a greater health hazard than marijuana.

However, some youngsters (users as well as nonusers) qualify their vote in this regard by observing, in effect, that while the perils of alcohol abuse are well known, there has not been enough testing done with marijuana to determine with certainty whether it is or is not dangerous to health.

Teens Driving While High

A startling one teenage driver out of eight, or 13 percent, says that he or she has driven a car or other motor vehicle while "high" from smoking marijuana. This marginally exceeds the 10 percent of teen drivers who admit having driven when they had had too much to drink.

Each of these forms of highly dangerous highway behavior is far more likely to have been practiced by teenage boys than girls. Almost one boy driver in five, 18 percent, told the latest Gallup Youth Survey that he had driven when under the influence of marijuana, while eight percent of girl drivers said that they had done so. Similarly, one out of seven boy drivers (14 percent) admitted that he had operated a motor vehicle after overindulging in an alcoholic beverage. For girl drivers the comparable figure is six percent.

It should be noted that the National Safety Council has estimated that approximately one-half of all highway fatalities, many of which involve teenagers, are related to the use of alcohol. There is also a consensus among experts that the risk of auto accidents increases with marijuana use, with a magnitude probably equal to that of alcohol.

The comments of young people who have and who have not

driven while intoxicated indicate that while both groups are aware of the grim statistics associated with the practice, the minority who have been guilty of these crimes apparently believe either that the urgency of their mission warranted driving while influenced by alcohol or marijuana, or felt that the extent of their intoxication was not serious enough to keep them from driving.

The majority of teen drivers, who have neither smoked nor drunk to excess while driving, have articulate spokesmen and spokeswomen. A 16-year-old boy commented:

"I feel that driving is a big responsibility, and that a driver must be a responsible, rational, physically-alert person."

These feelings are echoed by an 18-year-old boy:

"I can't believe people are stupid enough to get behind the wheel if they are not in control of their senses!"

The comments of this 17-year-old girl are not atypical:

"I wasn't out of control of anything, but it was enough to impair my judgment. Afterwards, I realized this, and told myself I wouldn't do it again (and I haven't, either)."

Another respondent, an 18-year-old boy, had this to say:

"I know too many people who have gotten into serious accidents after drinking or smoking. I would never drive if I thought I wasn't able. When I've smoked and driven, I'm extra cautious about speed limits, etc."

Aside from the marked differences between boys and girls in the incidence of driving while high, it is interesting to note that it appears to be less widespread among teenagers whose academic work is above average.

The standard indicators of social and economic class, such as parents' education and occupation, show no significant differences in the practices.

Teenage drivers living in the South are less likely to have driven while influenced by either alcohol or marijuana than those living in other areas of the country, but this is felt to be, at least in part, a function of lower incidences of teen drinking and marijuana smoking there.

The same observation may be made about teens living in urban areas (both in central cities and the suburbs) vs. essentially rural, nonurban areas. The incidence of driving while intoxicated in rural areas is low, but so too is the use of either alcohol or marijuana.

Marijuana:
Will It Be LEGALIZED?

If the American people were participating in a nationwide referendum, they would vote against legalizing the use of marijuana, but at the same time would remove criminal penalties for possession of small amounts of "grass."

In a recently completed Gallup Poll, two persons in three, 66 percent, voted against legalizing the use of marijuana while about one in three, 28 percent, favors legalization.

However, the public is ready to decriminalize marijuana. A majority, 53 percent, feels possession of small amounts of the substance should not be treated as a criminal offense, while 41 percent would retain criminal penalties.

Presently, eight states have decriminalized "pot," that is, made possession of small amounts (generally an ounce or less) a civil offense, much like a traffic ticket.

Support for decriminalization is found in all major population groups with the exception of Southerners, those over 50 years old, and people whose education ended at the grade-school level.

In the vanguard of support for decriminalization are the young and the college-educated. Among these two groups nearly seven in ten support more lenient pot laws.

Of the eight states that have changed their laws, four are in the West; thus it is no surprise that people living in this region (and those living in the East) are most likely to favor removing criminal penalties for possessing small quantities of grass. Midwesterners and Southerners are closely divided—the former lean in favor of decriminalization, and the latter lean in opposition.

Here is the question asked to determine attitudes toward removing criminal penalties for possession of small amounts of marijuana:

"So you think the possession of small amounts of marijuana should or should not be treated as a criminal offense?"

Following are the national results as well as the findings by key population groups:

Should Possession of Small Amounts of Marijuana Be a Criminal Offense?

	Should	Should not	No opinion
NATIONAL	41%	53%	6%
Men	38%	56%	6%
Women	44%	50%	6%
College	25%	69%	6%
High school	46%	49%	5%
Grade school	55%	37%	8%
East	33%	60%	7%
Midwest	45%	50%	5%
South	50%	44%	6%
West	33%	61%	6%
Under 30 years old	29%	68%	3%
30-49 years old	45%	51%	4%
50 years & older	48%	43%	9%
Have tried marijuana	14%	85%	1%
Never tried marijuana	50%	43%	7%
Marijuana physically harmful	60%	34%	6%
Marijuana habit-forming	59%	36%	5%
Marijuana leads to hard drugs	62%	33%	5%

Legalization Support Growing

Although Americans still heavily oppose legalizing the use of marijuana—that is, removing all penalties, even small fines—the latest findings represent a continuing erosion in the opposition to legalization. In 1973, the public voted against legalization, 78-16 percent. In 1969, the comparable figures were 84-12 percent.

Here is the question asked to determine attitudes toward legalizing marijuana and the trend since 1969:

Do you think the use of marijuana should be made legal?

	Yes	No	No opinion
TODAY	28%	66%	6%
1973	16%	78%	6%
1972	15%	81%	4%
1969	12%	84%	4%

Among the major population groups, only young people can be said to favor legalizing marijuana. With other groups, opinion on the subject follows the same pattern found with regard to decriminalization—the college-educated (and young) are most favorably inclined; people with a grade-school educational background and older people are most opposed.

Regional patterns hold, with inhabitants of the far West and East most likely to favor legalization—Southerners and Midwesterners most likely to oppose it.

People who have tried marijuana support removing all penalties by a 3-to-1 vote, while those who have not tried it oppose such a step by the same ratio.

The findings also suggest that some of the opposition to legalized grass can be traced to perceptions regarding marijuana's effects. Among those who believe it has a deleterious effect on one's health, the vote against legalization ranges from 7-to-1 to 10-to-1.

Teens Oppose Legalization

By a substantial two-to-one ratio (62 to 32 percent), American teenagers oppose legalizing the use of marijuana.

At the same time, however, they feel, by a smaller 54 to 42 percent margin, that being found with small amounts of "pot" on their person should not be treated as a crime.

The rationale behind this sentiment is demonstrated by these comments of a 16-year-old girl who admits to smoking pot "at a party every once in a while."

"I feel that it's just another vice that society can really do without. Just like alcohol, if it is legalized, more people will use it than if it's illegal and therefore harder to get. But as for getting locked up just because you've got a joint in your purse—that's almost like a police state.''

As important as are these national findings from a recent Gallup Youth Survey, the attitudes of various *segments* of the teenage population are perhaps equally so.

Most obvious are the differences in opinions of those teens who have tried marijuana vs. those who have never used it. Not surprisingly, teens who have smoked at one time or another are far more likely to feel that the use of pot should be made legal (59 percent) than teens who haven't tried the drug (14 percent).

Similarly, while only 18 percent of past or present pot smokers believe that simple possession should be treated as a criminal offense, fully 58 percent of nonusers feel this way.

Boys are more likely to be or to have been pot smokers than girls and are also somewhat more permissive toward its legal use and possession.

The fact that younger teens (13 to 15 years old) of both sexes are far more likely to hold conservative viewpoints on each of these questions—to oppose legal use and to favor criminal prosecution for possession—is primarily a function of use, since twice as many 16 to 18 year olds (52 percent) have tried marijuana than have their 13 to 15-year-old counterparts (26 percent). Older teenagers are also apt to be more frequent users: 22 percent of older teens smoked during the month prior to the survey while only nine percent of younger teens did so.

As is the case with so many questions involving socially-sensitive behavior, teens who live in the East and the far West exhibit the most tolerant attitudes toward the legality of marijuana possession and use. Teens living in these areas are also more likely to have tried marijuana and to have done so more recently.

Finally, those whose school work is above average are less likely to be or to have been pot users than teens whose school work is less than outstanding. However, the attitudes of the two groups on the questions regarding legality are virtually identical.

Of the total teenage sample, 40 percent say that they have tried marijuana at some point in their lives. This projects to approximately ten million American teenagers.

Marijuana's Relationship to HARD DRUGS

Despite the efforts of pro-marijuana groups, most of the public continues to see "grass" as a pernicious, habit-forming substance that ultimately leads to use of harder drugs.

In a recently completed Gallup Poll, majorities of the public agree not only that it is physically harmful (55 percent) and addictive (59 percent), but also that it leads to hard drugs (59 percent) such as heroin.

While these findings are doubtless discouraging to marijuana advocates, the percentage of Americans who believe the substance is harmful (down 11 points) and who think it leads to hard drug use (down 16 points) have both declined significantly since 1972. The percentage who believe it is physically addictive has remained at about the same level as recorded in 1972.

Remarkable Consistency

Analysis of the findings for all three questions—is marijuana physically harmful, is it habit-forming, does it lead to hard drug use—reveals sharp contrasts in attitudes by sex, education, age, and region of the nation.

Opinion by each of these population groups is generally the same on all three questions. For example:

109

- Men are more likely to agree with the pro-marijuana viewpoint on all questions than are women;

- The higher the education of the respondent, the more likely one is to hold a pro-marijuana viewpoint. In all three cases, those with only a grade-school education are the most conservative in their beliefs, with the high-school educated falling between;

- Younger adults (under 30) are most likely to have a pro-marijuana viewpoint with the 30-49-year-old group significantly more antimarijuana, and those over 50 years old most convinced of its harmful qualities;

- People living in the Northeast and far West are more apt, on all three questions, to have a pro-marijuana viewpoint than are Midwesterners and Southerners.

User, Abstainer Viewpoints

Analysis of the views of persons who have tried marijuana reveals a not unexpected consistency. Those who have never tried marijuana are, in all three cases, more likely to accept the antimarijuana view than are users. And among users alone, those whose contact with the substance was more than one year ago have uniformly more anti-marijuana views than current users.

Here are the three questions asked in the survey:
"Please tell me whether you agree or disagree with each of the following statements: For most people the use of marijuana is physically harmful. For most people marijuana is physically addictive or habit forming. For most people the use of marijuana leads to the use of hard drugs."

And here, for each question, is a comparison of the latest results with those recorded in 1972 followed by the results by key population groups:

Marijuana Physically Harmful?

	Agree	Disagree	No Opinion
TODAY	55%	33%	12%
1972	66%	25%	9%

	Agree	Disagree	No Opinion	Change in 'agree' since 1972
NATIONAL	55%	33%	12%	− 11%
Men	48%	41%	11%	− 11%
Women	61%	27%	12%	− 11%
College	41%	51%	8%	− 8%
High school	59%	30%	11%	− 8%
Grade school	71%	11%	18%	− 13%
East	50%	37%	13%	− 12%
Midwest	58%	31%	11%	− 7%
South	61%	27%	12%	− 14%
West	50%	42%	8%	− 10%
Under 30 years old	34%	60%	6%	− 12%
30-49 years old	55%	33%	12%	− 9%
50 years and older	72%	13%	15%	− 11%
Have tried marijuana	18%	77%	5%	*
During the last year	10%	89%	1%	*
More than a year ago	24%	67%	9%	*
Have never tried marijuana	67%	20%	13%	*

* Comparative data not available

Marijuana Physically Addictive?

	Agree	Disagree	No Opinion
TODAY	59%	30%	11%
1972	61%	27%	12%

	Agree	Disagree	No Opinion	Change in 'agree' since 1972
NATIONAL	59%	30%	11%	− 2%
Men	53%	36%	11%	− 1%
Women	65%	24%	11%	− 2%
College	38%	47%	15%	− 2%
High school	63%	27%	10%	− 1%
Grade school	83%	7%	10%	even
East	54%	36%	10%	− 4%
Midwest	62%	28%	10%	+ 3%
South	63%	21%	16%	− 5%
West	54%	37%	9%	− 1%
Under 30 years old	35%	59%	6%	− 2%
30-49 years old	60%	27%	13%	+ 1%
50 years and older	77%	9%	14%	− 1%
Have tried marijuana	23%	72%	5%	*
During the last year	10%	88%	2%	*
More than a year ago	32%	63%	5%	*
Have never tried marijuana	70%	17%	13%	*

* Comparative data not available

Marijuana Lead to Hard Drugs?

	Agree	Disagree	No Opinion
TODAY	59%	31%	10%
1972	75%	17%	8%

	Agree	Disagree	No Opinion	Change in 'agree' since 1972
NATIONAL	59%	31%	10%	−16%
Men	52%	38%	10%	−19%
Women	66%	25%	9%	−14%

112

	Agree	Disagree	No Opinion	Change in 'agree' since 1972
College	40%	50%	10%	−17%
High school	64%	27%	9%	−14%
Grade school	81%	8%	11%	− 7%
East	53%	38%	9%	−20%
Midwest	62%	28%	10%	−16%
South	68%	22%	10%	−14%
West	52%	39%	9%	−14%
Under 30 years old	37%	58%	5%	−23%
30-49 years old	61%	29%	10%	−14%
50 years and older	76%	11%	13%	−10%
Have tried marijuana	20%	76%	4%	*
During the last year	5%	91%	4%	*
More than a year ago	30%	65%	5%	*
Have never tried marijuana	72%	17%	11%	*

* Comparative data not available

ALCOHOLISM

The proportion of Americans who say that liquor has been a cause of trouble in their families has doubled in just four years.

Alcohol's Effect on Family Life

Currently, one person in four (24 percent) says an alcohol-related problem has adversely affected his or her family life. The number in 1974 was 12 percent. The uptrend since 1974 is recorded among most major socioeconomic groups and in all regions of the nation.

The porportion saying liquor has been a cause of trouble is as high as one-third among persons in the study who are separated or divorced.

The current study was undertaken by the Gallup Poll in close cooperation with David C. Hancock of Prevention of Alcohol Problems, Inc., Minneapolis, Minnesota, and David A. Works of the North Conway Institute, Boston, Massachusetts.

Overindulgence has increased.

The study also reveals that the proportion of Americans who admit to overindulgence on occasion has increased sharply from 18 percent one year ago to 23 percent today.

Men are far more likely than are women to say they sometimes drink to excess. In addition, persons with higher incomes and/or a higher level of formal education are the most likely to say they sometimes drink more than they think they should.

High Percentage of Drinkers

The percentage of adult drinkers (18 and older) remains at the same level as last year—the highest percentage recorded in nearly four decades.

The latest nationwide drinking audit shows 71 percent of adults saying they use alcoholic beverages such as liquor, wine, or beer. Only 29 percent are total abstainers.

The highest proportion of drinkers is found among men, younger persons, higher income groups, those living outside the South, professional and business people, and persons with a college background.

Teenage Drinking: A Serious Problem

Teenage drinking is causing particular concern among experts and parents alike. A Gallup survey conducted for the Charles F. Kettering Foundation revealed 55 percent of parents saying they believed drinking to be a "serious" problem among youth in their communities. And an overwhelming 84 percent favored a required school course on the effects of alcohol and drugs.

Teenagers, themselves, name alcohol as one of the three most serious problems facing their generation, as revealed by a Gallup Youth Survey. In addition, more than one-third of drinking teens (36 percent) say they sometimes drink more than they should. Among older teens (16 to 18 years old) the figure reaches 43 percent.

Number One Health Problem

The current study of the "Problem Drinker in American society" takes a careful and revealing look at problem drinking in American society, often called America's number one health problem.

Social observers have expressed alarm at excessive drinking and alcoholism in American society, pointing to findings that show alcohol to be involved in about half of highway fatalities and about half of all homicides. The abuse of alcohol also is a contributing factor to divorce, broken homes, and child abuse, as well as a host of other problems.

The "Problem Drinker"

While most studies have focused on the alcoholic, the current study represents an effort to probe the behavior and attitudes of the "problem drinker." In the current study, each survey respondent was asked a series of 20 questions adapted from a list developed by the National Council on Alcoholism, Los Angeles County, Inc.

The 20 questions range from "Do you drink to build up your self-confidence?" to "Is drinking affecting your reputation or jeopardizing your job?" to "Have you ever been to a hospital or arrested due to drinking?"

If the survey respondent answers two or more of 20 questions affirmatively, it could be an indication of problem drinking.

The Study's Results

The results of the current study show that a total of 25 percent of the total sample say "yes" to at least one or more of the 20 questions, with 14 percent saying "yes" to one question, and the remaining 11 percent saying "yes" to two or more questions.

Among drinkers, a total of 35 percent say "yes" to at least one of the 20 questions, with 20 percent saying "yes" to one question, and the remaining 11 percent saying "yes" to two or more questions.

SOCIAL DRINKING

Alcoholic beverages are served in the homes of about one out of five American teenagers when they get together for a party with their friends.

And as many as one-fourth of the teens who do offer beer, wine, or hard liquor at their parties say their friends would be less likely to come if these beverages were not served.

The latest Gallup Youth Survey also found that alcohol plays an even more significant role in the social life of certain subgroups of the teenage population.

For example, alcoholic beverages are served at about one-third (34 percent) of 16 to 18-year-old teenagers' parties whereas the figure for younger teens (13 to 15-year-olds) is 10 percent.

Whether a teenager's parents are drinkers themselves has an important bearing on whether alcohol is served at teen parties. In 29 percent of homes where the parents drink, alcoholic beverages are likely to be served, while this is true in the homes of only 13 percent of teens whose parents are abstainers.

Not surprisingly, whether or not teenagers drink alcoholic beverages themselves is the most important factor in determining whether alcohol is served at their parties. In 45 percent of the homes of teens who are drinkers, alcohol is usually served at parties, whereas in only 8 percent of non-drinkers' homes is this the case.

The comments of two survey participants illustrate the two basic underlying and conflicting attitudes toward entertaining with or without alcoholic drinks.

"Why else would they come? My friends wouldn't come because the party probably wouldn't be any fun. Anyway, if they knew I wasn't going to have anything, they would bring their own or we would smoke"—18-year-old boy.

"My friends know I don't drink, so they don't expect any liquor when they come to my house. Besides, if your friends won't come unless there's liquor, they're really not worth having"—14-year-old junior-high-school girl.

In addition to the major differences by age, their own and their parents' use or nonuse of alcohol noted above, boys are somewhat more likely to offer alcoholic beverages at their parties than are girls, and boys who do serve these beverages are more inclined than girls to feel that their friends would be less likely to come if alcoholic drinks weren't available.

Another question in the survey sought to determine what types of alcoholic beverages are served in teens' homes which offer these beverages at all. While it will surprise few readers that beer is far and away the favorite beverage—served at almost nine out of 10 (87 percent) teen parties where alcohol is served—the extent to which wine and hard liquor are offered may startle some. At as many as one teen party in four in homes where alcoholic beverages are served, wine and/or hard liquor are offered as well as beer, or, in a small minority of such homes (13 percent), are served instead of beer. Again, the age of the teens involved is an important determinant.

Among older teens who offer any kind of alcoholic beverages at their parties, three out of ten (30 percent) at least sometimes serve hard liquor; the comparable figure for younger teens is 16 percent.

Finally, the survey studied the peer relationships between drinking teenagers and those who do not drink.

When asked what proportion of their close friends drink alcoholic beverages, almost two out of three teenagers (64 percent) who drink claimed that most of their close friends are also drinkers. Only one out of nine (11 percent) of nondrinking teens said that most of their friends, unlike themselves, drink. Conversely, while 11 percent of drinking teenagers say hardly any or none of their close friends drink, 63 percent of teetotalling youngsters make the same claim.

118

Following are the questions asked and the principal survey findings:

"When you have a party with friends in your own home, are alcoholic beverages usually served, or not?"

Percent Serving Alcoholic Beverages

| | Total Sample | Teens Whose Parents | |
		Drink	Don't Drink
NATIONWIDE	22%	29%	13%
Boys	24%	31%	16%
Girls	20%	27%	11%
Both sexes			
13-15 yrs. old	10%	13%	7%
16-18 yrs. old	34%	44%	20%

Do you think your friends would be less likely to come if you did not serve alcoholic beverages?

	Less Likely	No Difference	Not Sure
NATIONWIDE	26%	72%	2%
Boys	28%	70%	2%
Girls	23%	74%	3%
Both sexes			
13-15 yrs. old	24%	73%	3%
16-18 yrs. old	27%	72%	1%

NOTE: Based on those teenagers in whose homes alcohol is served at parties.

TEENS and the Drinking Problem

"After my father died, my mother began drinking heavily. That was bad enough, but my older brother made the problem worse by getting drunk himself and lashing out at my mother"—17-year-old boy, high-school junior.

"When I was 13 or 14, I started hanging around with a group of kids who thought it was 'cool' to drink. At first, it was just beer, but then we had to try other stuff. Before long, we were getting loaded just about every weekend. Some of the kids got into some real bad trouble because of drinking—accidents and stuff like that"—16-year-old girl, high-school sophomore.

The comments of these two teenagers illustrate two different dimensions of alcohol-related family problems mentioned in the latest Gallup Youth Survey by (nearly) one teenager in five (18 percent), who said that liquor had been a cause of trouble in his or her family.

Other survey questions reveal that:

Almost four teenagers in ten (37 percent) at least occasionally drink some form of alcohol, with the proportion rising to as high as six out of ten (60 percent) in the case of 16 to 18-year-old boys. Even among the youngest boys and girls surveyed (13 to 15-year-olds) one in five (21 percent) is a drinker.

Teenagers whose parents drink are more than two and a half

times as likely to drink themselves (52 percent) as teens whose parents are abstainers (19 percent). This is particularly true in the case of younger teens of both sexes, nonwhites, teens from Protestant homes, those living in the South and, to a lesser extent, teens from blue-collar families. In each of these groups, teenagers are relatively unlikely to drink if their parents do not drink.

More than one-third of drinking teens (36 percent) say they sometimes drink more than they should. Among younger teenager drinkers, 19 percent make the same claim, while the figure for 16-to-18-year-olds is 43 percent.

Not surprisingly, the favorite alcoholic beverage is beer, but about one in five of older teens (18 percent) occasionally drinks wine or hard liquor as well.

Three out of four 13-to-15-year-old drinkers (74 percent) say their parents are aware of their drinking. The figure for 16-to-18-year-old drinkers is 87 percent.

Dr. Gail Gleason Milgram, Director of Education of the Center of Alcohol Studies at Rutgers University, commented about these Gallup Youth Survey findings:

"It is extremely important that teenagers be aware of the reality of teenage drinking so that they may clarify their values related to drinking, and make decisions based on accurate information rather than assumptions about what other teenagers are doing. This will enable teenagers to discuss drinking with their peers, and openly identify alternatives to minimize the risks related to drinking. An accurate perspective of the facts of teenage drinking also identifies nondrinking as a viable alternative."

Following are other survey highlights:

Although, as mentioned earlier, 18 percent of the total teenage sample cite a family problem related to the use of alcohol, among teens whose parents are drinkers, the figure rises to 24 percent. In homes where the parents do not drink, it is 10 percent. In a 1976 Gallup Poll of the nation's adult population, the same proportion (18 percent) said that alcohol had been a cause of family problems.

Drinking problems are somewhat more apt to be mentioned by teenagers who come from blue-collar rather than white-collar families, and are considerably more likely to occur in homes where the teens' parents are divorced.

There are proportionally more white teenagers who drink alcoholic beverages (40 percent) than nonwhites who do so (25 percent).

121

The lowest incidence of teenage drinking is found in the South (30 percent).

When the proportions of teenagers who sometimes overindulge are examined by the different socioeconomic groups to which they belong, very few important differences are found, except by age.

Following are the questions asked and the principal findings:

Do you sometimes drink more than you think you should?

| | Asked of Drinkers: | |
	Yes	No
NATIONWIDE	36%	64%
Boys	39%	61%
Girls	34%	66%
Both Sexes:		
13-15 yrs. old	19%	81%
16-18 yrs. old	43%	57%

Has liquor ever been a cause of trouble in your family?

| | Percent Answering "YES" | |
	Total Sample	Teens who drink
NATIONWIDE	18%	26%
Boys	17%	25%
Girls	19%	27%
Both sexes:		
13-15 yrs. old	13%	20%
16-18 yrs. old	23%	28%

Why CHILDREN Drink

It is not difficult to see why alcohol abuse has become one of the nation's most serious problems. A recent Gallup study on the problem drinker in American society reveals the following:

• As many as one-half of all parents say they set no guidelines regarding the use of alcoholic beverages by their children. (An earlier survey showed four parents in ten failing to do so in the case of their teenagers.)

• One drinker in ten admits that his or her pattern of alcohol use would not be a good model for his or her children to follow, while another 15 percent express uncertainty, or do not offer an opinion.

In this respect, it is interesting to note that about half of all drinkers say they have no specific rules or guidelines regarding their *own* use of alcoholic beverages.

• About one person in 12 believes there to be no risk involved with the regular use of alcohol, while another 16 percent express uncertainty, or do not give an opinion.

• About one person in six says he or she would not know where or to whom to turn for help in the event someone in his or her family had a drinking problem.

America faces a serious drinking problem. As reported in chapter one, one person in four (24 percent) says an alcohol-related problem has adversely affected his or her family life. The figure in 1974 was 12 percent. In addition, the proportion of Americans who admit to overindulgence on occasion has increased sharply from 18 percent one year ago to 23 percent today. (The current percentage is 34 percent among drinkers.)

The current study was undertaken by the Gallup Poll in close cooperation with David C. Hancock of Prevention of Alcohol Problems, Inc., Minneapolis, and David A. Works of the North Conway Institute, Boston.

Following are the questions that were asked of parents:

Do you have any specific rules or guidelines regarding your own use of alcoholic beverages?

Practice moderation	24%
One or two drink limit	7%
Drink only on certain occasions	4%
Don't drink to get drunk	4%
Know when to stop	3%
Never drink before noon or during day	2%
No drinking if I'm driving	2%
Other responses	4%
None/no guidelines	47%
Don't know/no answer	3%
	100%

Do you have any guidelines regarding the use of alcoholic beverages by your children?

Not allowed to drink. No liquor allowed in home	21%
Moderation	10%
Not allowed to drink until of age	9%
May drink only in home	3%
No drinking and driving	2%
No rules	51%
No opinion/no answer	4%
	100%

Do you feel that your pattern of alcohol use would be a good model for your children to follow, or not?

Yes	75%
No	10%
No opinion	15%
	100%

Do you think there are any risks involved with the regular use of alcohol?

Could become addicted to, or dependent upon alcohol	34%
Could ruin one's health	26%
Drunken driving	9%
Damages liver	9%
Could cause brain cell deterioration	7%
Causes abnormal behavior, makes one accident-prone	7%
Other responses	10%
No, none	8%
No opinion/no answer	16%
	131%*

*Total adds to more than 100 percent due to multiple responses.

If you or someone else in your family had a drinking problem, where or to whom would you turn for help?

Alcoholics Anonymous	42%
God/the Lord/prayer/the Bible	9%
Priest, minister, rabbi	8%
The church and its trained personnel	8%
Doctor	7%
Family member	6%
Counseling, local treatment center	5%

Hospital	3%
Friend	3%
Other responses	2%
No one	4%
Don't know/no answer	16%
	113%*

*Total adds to more than 100 percent due to multiple responses.

There are encouraging developments on several fronts:
1. A growing number of organizations with job-related alcohol programs.
2. A sobering up among many American motorists, according to the National Highway Safety Administration, which attributes the trend to increasing law enforcement, rehabilitation, and educational efforts.
3. A decline in deaths from cirrhosis of the liver.
4. An apparent trend toward the consumption of nonalcoholic beverages at lunches and cocktail parties.
5. An apparent levelling out in the proportion of American adults and teenagers who say liquor has been a cause of trouble in their homes.
6. The continuing and remarkable work of Alcoholics Anonymous. It has been said that the birth of Alcoholics Anonymous and its growth through the western world to more than a million members is one of the sociological phenomena of our times.
7. A growing interest among parents in working closely with teachers in a team effort to deal with such problems as discipline, drug and alcohol abuse.
8. The desire on the part of the overwhelming majority of Americans (more than nine in ten) for the public schools in their areas to provide instruction in the area of alcohol and drug abuse. There would appear to be a growing awareness among the American people in regard to what is called "the alcohol problem," and at the same time a growing desire to get on top of this problem.

We still face an uphill battle which will take the concerted efforts of teachers, doctors, the media, concerned Christians, and, most of all, parents to deal with a problem that is having a serious drain on society.

Many believe that the best place to launch a campaign against the destructive influence of alcohol in our society is in the home.

In this respect it behooves parents to (1) pay heed to their own drinking habits; (2) set the proper example of pursuing higher and more lasting values than those embodied in drug dependency; (3) be aware of their children's drinking habits; (4) talk to their children about drinking and the potential dangers (As many as four in ten do not presently do so!); and (5) encourage their offspring to look at the use of alcohol from a religious perspective.

More books for your reading enjoyment

Adventures in Being a Parent/Family Enrichment Ideas for Busy Parents by Shirley Pollock. True anecdotes that will provide a few chuckles along with some practical suggestions for enriching your family life. 144 pages. No. 2971, $3.95.

Reaching Out With Love/Encounters With Troubled Youth by Jean Marie Campbell. Demonstrates the dramatic possibilities of applied Christianity in reaching kids with problems—teenage pregnancy, drugs, low motivation, stealing, lying, aggressiveness toward authority. 144 pages. No. 3652, $3.95

What Do You Do With Joe? by Elizabeth W. Crisci. Shows how tactful teachers and parents can help problem youngsters—Bashful Barb, Turned-off Terry, Know-it-all Norm, Silly Sally, Doubting Dick—be the persons God wants them to be. 64 pages. No. 3650, $2.75.

Listen to Your Children by Marie Frost. Positive principles for nurturing children by creative listening, establishing authority, and following Scriptural truths. 144 pages. No. 3000, $2.50.

The Power of the Christian Woman by Phyllis Schlafly. A portrait of the Christian woman as she faces such contemporary, sometimes controversial, issues as marriage and motherhood, careers, divorce, ERA, etc. 256 pages. No. 2972, $4.95.

Frankly Feminine/God's Idea of Womanhood by Gloria Hope Hawley. Comes to grips with such vital issues as communication in marriage, gender dichotomy, emotional disturbances, priorities, and afflictions in the light of God's Word and will. 128 pages. No. 2969, $3.50.

People of Destiny by Roger Elwood. Twenty-three nationally-known Christians speak out on subjects of major concern to all thoughtful Americans. 184 pages, casebound. No. 5000, $9.95.

Turning Point by Roger Elwood. Over a dozen recognized Christian leaders address such tough questions as church and family, government and education, and right and wrong, in relation to the quality of life in the next decade. 200 pages, casebound. No. 5001, $8.95.